Dear Students

Dear Students

Reading, Writing,
and the
Art of Smelling Books

* * *

Jennifer Gavin

Falls Books

Published by Falls Books

ISBN 978-1-9867-9914-0

Typesetting services by BOOKOW.COM

Dedicated to all of my students:
past, present, future, and hypothetical.
Even the ones I couldn't reach.

Contents

Introduction: Life Marked by Pages   1

I Dear Students   9

1   *The Problem of Reading*   11

2   *'Tis Common: Education Reform*   17

3   *Real Talk*   31

4   *Writing: Getting Bitter Before Getting Better*   33

5   *Movie Teachers*   41

6   *Losing Legends in the Details: Darth Vader and Writer's Block*   43

7   *It's Late, Not a Tsunami*   51

8   *Boccaccio, McCarthy, and the Compassion Cure*   55

9   *What You Need to Know About "Good Country People"*   63

10   *Patriot of the Active Voice*   69

11	*More on the Non-Reading Problem: Bluff-Busting*	75
12	*Embracing the Unknowing: Socratic Seminars, Featuring Two Fish Allusions*	77
13	Green Centuries, *Ray Bradbury, and the Necessity of Myth*	81
14	*Poetry Teacher Cleans out the Lost and Found*	89

II   Reading the World   91

15	*Soul-Depleting Narcissism and April's Epic Wound*	93
16	*What Will I Do with My Life? Hopefully, Many Things Having Nothing to Do with Each Other*	97
17	*Tartufo Man*	105
18	*Missing*	113
19	*Working Itself Out: Three Good Conversations and a Terrifying Plane Ride*	115
20	*Audrey Hepburn and Living Marble*	121
21	*Ubi Sunt? Or, Where Have All the Cowboys Gone?*	125
22	*Hysteria One, Discourse Zero*	133
23	*Not with a Bang, but with a Whimper*	137
24	*Seven*	141
25	*Super-Teachers and Euclid's Reluctant Hero*	143
26	*Down with the Research Paper*	155

Contents

27   *Why Dante?*   163

Conclusion: Advice for the Roads   167

III Appendix   **171**

Appendix A Educational Philosophy   173

Appendix B Plagiarism: ZERO TOLERANCE   175

Appendix C Reading Tips: Common Problems and Solutions   177

Appendix D Essay Comments: Elizabeth Bishop's "One Art"   179

Appendix E Dante and the Price of Beguiling Rhetoric   189

Acknowledgements   217

Introduction:
Life Marked by Pages

Let's go back to the dog-eared depths of nostalgia, back to the green-and-gold tinted days of early childhood, so I can tell you why I've loved books since long before I could read. I'll show you the very beginnings of a life marked by pages.

My first tactile attachment to an inanimate object in this world was not to a blanket or stuffed animal, but to a massive old tome that was perpetually drifting around our household. It was an illustrated compendium of *Lives of the Saints* and Dante's *Divine Comedy*. The corners of the volume had a light grainy taste, with the merest hint of pine. The cover lost its flavor over time, mellowing into a warped, soggy pulp.

In later years, I knew it would be perfect for Show and Tell. Standing up in front of the class, I pointed out the colorful illustrations, tortured saints with orange Technicolor faces and bright, electric-blue-rimmed robes glowing at high voltage.

My classmates were unimpressed by Saint Andrew, healer of sore throats and spinsterhood, and clearly yearned to pass around Timmy Conley's G.I. Joe. Long after they had gazed off into space, my kindergarten teacher smiled awkwardly and said, "Your family must draw a lot of strength from your religion." And I did.

The religion in our family was books. I was surrounded by them: volumes and volumes on shelves in every room. Paperbacks, hardcovers, classics, antiques. Poetry, Irish drama, detective novels. Short stories, true crime, gardening, theology, spy thrillers, historical romances. Geoffrey Chaucer, Richard Wright, Karl Marx, John Milton, Agatha Christie, Spinoza, Alexander Pope, Dr. Seuss, Eugene O'Neill, Evelyn Waugh, Betty Friedan. Madeline L'Engle, Donald Sobel, Gordan Korman, James Clavell, Mark Twain, Victoria Holt. Ogden Nash, Richard Scarry, Aleksandr Solzhenitsyn, James Baldwin, John LeCarre, Arthur Conan Doyle, Dorothy Parker. Alice Walker, Shel Silverstein, Marcus Aurelius, Isaac Bashevis Singer. Judy Blume, Beverly Cleary, Jonathan Swift, Francine Pascal, Caroline B. Cooney, Paula Danziger. Our shelves contained multitudes; many of them were filled with what I knew to be my mother's handwriting.

We often ask what we can do to get kids to read; there's such a dramatic fall-off of reading once they hit the tween years. I have many ideas, but no one easy answer. For one thing, it's a societal tarnish that the blessing of a reading environment is not granted to everyone. My own upbringing may have been unconventional, but everything in my life drew me to learning. I was fortunate to be raised in such a story-rich, book-saturated home. If it helps, I can show you all what that looked like.

My father read to us every night. Tacitly we absorbed the concrete fact that reading together inclined us toward something greater than ourselves. Books were all proof of a cosmos whose entirety was far beyond our ken. Peering into books, my father and I would catch glimpses behind the veil into an asomatous domain, the one to which artists beckon us, if we just kept on reading and talking about books. He'd walk us through issues of the *New Yorker* and we'd tell stories about the people in the ads. "Now here we have a very fashionable woman. She's leaning with her hands in her pocket, just wondering about things. What is she thinking about? Where does she work? Why did she wear a brown suit today?"

Nothing was as satisfying as the smell of books. Reading required full absorption, demanding to be cherished by every possible sense of being in this world. When it came to books, I wished there were a way to breathe and ingest them. A book's tangibility and texture were inseparable from the story itself. Huck Finn's adventures unfolded in a mass market paperback, and if I had first read about them on anything other than that earthy, sun-bleached paper, they would've emanated a cold, antiseptic sterility. Conversely, I could only enjoy Jane Austen if it were on digest-size acid-free paper stock.

Give me the essence of ink and pulp. At the bookstore, I always did the smell test. Was the paper woodsy? Glossy? Did it have a robust, doughy finish? To me, books smelled like coming home. Chanel No. 5? No. Imagine: a splash of Eau-de-Livre behind the ears, and a dainty dab on the wrist. Fragrance industry, you're welcome.

My strict grandmother, mother of eight, had been a schoolteacher devoted to education, but my book obsession only pleased her so much. She was disturbed by my ritual of plunging my face into the center of a book and inhaling theatrically. Ominously, she intoned, "I knew a girl who lost brain cells from doing that." She always knew a-girl-who.

Feeling like a disappointing infidel, I tried my best to stop. I really did. But I simply had to mash my nostrils into a book and breathe deeply, to the basement of my existence, whenever Anne Shirley cracked a slate over Gilbert Blythe's head, Danny and his father became champions of the world, and, especially, when the Giving Tree let herself be chopped down.

A love of reading, an awareness of the world of literature, enriches our lives and beckons us to something beautiful. To read is to learn constantly, fueled by the interdisciplinary connections that make isolated galaxies of knowledge a little more attainable. Active readers come to realize that Orwell and Dante are, in their own ways, both trying to reach the same thing. We must train ourselves to crave these sublime glimpses beyond the veil of the ordinary. And, because we are all brother-keepers, we must reach out to others, stoking each other's curiosity and bonding over the truths we cannot touch.

I grew up understanding that there is more than one way to gnaw on a book, so it would be hard to pinpoint one explicit moment when I learned the importance of literacy. It was just a given in our household, starting with an inkling that flourished into a mode of living and permeated my entire being. You couldn't escape it. Who would want to?

The culture of education in our home was hardly lip service. Dad always reminded us that his grandfather, who came from nothing, had put three daughters through college during the Great Depression. I can't imagine what deprivations he shouldered to make that happen and defy the era's skepticism: Women? In college? *During the Depression?* One of the three sisters became president of the College of New Rochelle. Another taught English and married a principal. My grandmother, the third, who would later worry about my book-smelling routine, became a teacher at Waverly Elementary School in Tuckahoe, New York.

Despite growing up in a household without a mother, my sister and I absorbed the conviction that there were things far greater and far more beautiful than our pedestrian joys and woes. We told stories and talked about books constantly. Going to the bookstore as a family was a special treat so exciting that it nearly made me pass out. Still does. Delight was guaranteed and safeguarded by the loving care of my father, a widower: working late, coming home tired from a stressful government job, and sitting down to read books to his two small daughters.

We can proclaim, individually and as a culture, what we prioritize. We can declare our principles all we want. (And we certainly love to do it!) But it is only our actions that reveal what we truly value and who we are. My dad prized learning and literacy, starting with those glowing, nascent days of becoming. He never had to say so.

The millennium finds us all hopelessly modern. Numbed by sensory overload and lost in a chaotic melee of signs and symbols, our brains shut down and fixate on the immediate. We become complacent and passively accept scrolling information and flashing images washing over us. Pop culture icons, neon-flashing buttons, and half thoughts pulse through our consciousness. Our compulsive glances at our phones are not really focused inquiries about what time to meet someone for lunch, but anxious urges coming from a place deep within us that desires meaningful communion with other human beings.

The more we check for messages and notifications, the more we dodge and pine for this connection that we neither have nor understand, but desperately need to feel whole. We are left with the ultimate post-modernist image of a digital watch's momentary bleep: meaning nothing, coming from nothing, and gone forever.

Yet when we open a pulpy cover of a chewed-up book, we defy this meaninglessness. Welcome to the pains and pleasures of the universe, too infinite ever to be understood fully.

Every teacher thinks her subject is the most important. So it is with literature, which I consider the noblest realm of academia. Every year, I share my educational philosophy on the first day along with my take on plagiarism (see Appendices A and B); the philosophy supersedes the technicalities of the course.

It's imperative that we engage with books. We don't study English in lofty towers. We plunge ourselves into the earth, in the fertile soil of existence as mapped out on brittle parchment pages (a saucy blend: the scent of dust and oak, with a slightly crisp bouquet). In reading books, you are digging, toiling to get to the roots of human nature and the world, searching for the concrete basement of the universe upon which all human knowledge and experience depends.

I hope that throughout your lives, you nurture wonder in yourselves and others. So far, I've lived a life marked by and celebrated with pages. Within the course of these pages, maybe you will edge a little bit closer to doing the same. Part One of this book emphasizes reading, writing, and other topics related to the English classroom. Part Two widens the scope, addressing what reading and writing tell us about the world we live in today. My wish for you is that in reading the pages that lie ahead of you, both in this book and in the ones you have yet to live in your lives, you come closer to finding yourself in all the ways that matter. Keep reading. Ahead there.

J.A.G.

Dear Students

The Problem of Reading

Student:	(*Stomps around. Rolls eyes.*) I totally failed that chapter quiz!! And I read!!!! Ridiculous—how is anyone supposed to remember those little facts?
Friend:	Like the fact that the main character died and it took two long paragraphs to describe it?
Student:	PLEASE. That was just because I got home late and was tired at that point.
Friend:	But you were on the groupchat all night.
Student:	The thing is, I actually read!!
Friend:	You read SparkNotes.
Student:	But I actually *read* them. Same thing.

* * *

Dear Students,

Every student and teacher in the classroom is brought down by this: the non-reading problem. We all know the one, even if it isn't caused by each person. It varies from student to student. Maybe it's skimming, missing important points, and forgetting everything immediately. At least that's honest, as opposed to consulting poorly-written summaries. Don't fall into this damaging habit. It's nothing to be proud of.

A lot of us have been engaged in an elaborate game of fakery: you come to class pretending to have read, and I pretend not to notice. It's exhausting. It's far more important to your intellectual and innermost spiritual self to live genuinely. Imagine coming to school without that vague, sheepish anxiety because you haven't done what you were supposed to. Whether or not there's a reading quiz, you wonder if your teacher knows. (She does.) Suppose you truly earned every point. Envision comprehending the value of literacy, and embracing it. Imagine the moment when you catch yourself...enjoying reading. It's magical.

You'll have to read well in your lives, and pore over words closely. The worst thing to do is take the shortcuts, then tell yourself that you'll actually do the reading "when it counts." The problem with that is, when you need those reading skills, they just won't be there.

Online summaries like S@#%Notes are written at a fifth-grade reading level. The harsh truth: if you have been relying on them and never reading actual books, then that's where your reading is. It's no wonder if you then struggle with more challenging texts.

The best thing is to be honest. Resist the allure of the glowing screen that promises easy, quick answers—answers that, by the way, are often way off base. Know that those easy, quick answers provide data, but not wisdom. Now is the time. Carefully assess your skill and your effort. I am here to help you do just that. I will keep trying new things; you'll see. We will get there.

Most likely, your schedule is packed, but true literacy is a skill that just cannot be falsified in the world beyond. Everybody knows a faker. In English class, you are expected to work hard and honestly on improving your reading, writing, and critical thinking skills. Don't let yourself graduate without them. Don't kid yourself—you will need them no matter what you pursue in life.

What I am telling you doesn't apply to everyone. Maybe you're frustrated because you do the work and no one else does. The day reading is due, you dread an awkward, dull class, yearn for a good conversation, and brace yourself for being pestered by the slugs asking you to work with (meaning *for*) them. Maybe you die a little on the inside when the first thing a group member says is, "Did you read?" and guffaws with the other slackers who haven't. I see you. Hello and welcome. Because of course you need to read. It's no longer a question.

Read. Read everything you can. Novels, manga, magazines, poetry, toothpaste tubes. Street signs, newspapers, joke websites, recipes. If you've never read a book you've liked before, I apologize on behalf of a culture that has made you think there's no value or joy in reading. I get it; when you haven't ever read a good book, there's no way Melville is suddenly going to light your fire. We need to give you more choice in what you read. I never would have become an English teacher who treasures the classics if I hadn't started out with just reading what I liked, and a lot of it—shout-out to Ramona Quimby and the *Sweet Valley High* series (ask your parents).

You need to know this: nobody reading something for the first time understands everything. Nobody. That's natural. Be comfortable with not knowing, and trust that you're in good hands with the author. It will all come together.

Have you ever been in the movie theatre, and as soon as the film starts, someone in the audience loudly starts sharing their confusion?

"WHO'S THAT?! IS THAT THE GUY? WHERE IS HE GOING?! WHAT'S IN THAT PACKAGE HE'S CARRYING? THAT LOOKS HEAVY!"

You, however, sit there exasperated, because you know that you're not *supposed* to understand everything about the story in the first fifteen minutes. You trust that it's going somewhere. You accept it.

Reading is the same way; you've got to embrace the unknowing. Feeling bewildered doesn't mean that something is wrong or that you are not a good reader. Please read that sentence again. There are plenty of strategies to help you (see Appendix C for a start). I urge you to become comfortable and patient with yourselves as readers. Practice translating your confusion into intrigue.

I know that I'm in a profession that in many ways has become antiquated; what I ask you to do every day may as well be the equivalent of having you do calculus on an abacus. While I have grown grayer of late, I'm certainly no Gandalf, here to bar your way as I thunder, "YOU SHALL NOT PASS!"

You hear your teachers emphasize the importance of reading, but so little in your world validates this claim. The humanities aren't considered lucrative, high-profiled, or powerful. But they are real, they are profound, and they provide us with universal truths that are eternal. There's such joy and marvel waiting for you.

There are many reasons why students today just don't read the way they used to. We will talk about this throughout the year; I want to hear from you about this as well. Meanwhile, just be real. Give up any counterfeit swindles you may be pulling on yourself and others about your efforts and literacy. Authenticity takes work. I will help you and work alongside you fiercely. You will improve. It will be liberating.

Reading well is a complex cognitive process that makes all sorts of demands on your imagination, intellect, time, and concentration. Know that I don't believe everything in the media about "kids these days," and I pray that you are not trapped by the notions that others have of you. Each of you is capable of greatness that you can't possibly imagine. I will push you to do more than just get by. No hiding.

You each possess the potential to be epic. Together, we link arms and dive into the nihilistic abyss of modernity, returning with the elixir of life. We touch eternity. It is up to us to carry the fire, because we are the knights of the old order.

'Tis Common:
Education Reform

Elementary school teachers: Our kids aren't reading anymore.

Middle school teachers: Our kids can't and don't read.

High school teachers: Our kids can't and don't read.

Media: Why aren't these teachers teaching kids to read?! The system is broken!!!

Government: Whaaaaat?! We had no idea! Time for theorists and more tests!

Public K-12 teachers everywhere: (*Collective eye roll.*)

* * *

Dear Students,

Everybody has heard about the Common Core, and a lot of you have expressed your opinions. Maybe you have seen your younger siblings crying over their math homework while you and your parents stand by helplessly, befuddled about why calculations have to be so complicated. Maybe you've internalized the frisson over test scores that palpably buzzes within your parents and teachers. A few years ago, I was asked what I thought about the Common Core curriculum, and I wrote a candid reply. Now, several exams in, and having changed my mind about a few things, here are some thoughts.

Education is supposed to inspire children to imagine, think creatively, discover their strengths, and give them skills to solve problems. In many ways, the fixation on testing undermines these goals. Aligning standards is necessary, and maybe I'm only nettled because I envy people who get paid to write curriculum. That's what I do for fun when I'm not teaching. Put me in a room with a book and my Syntopicon, and don't talk to me for three days. I will make it happen. Dream job!

The Common Core's concentration is now "informational texts," that is, nonfiction that may or may not be literary. Its aim is to have students read for information, not for subtleties in language, subtext, or—heaven forbid—joy.

I've had so many conversations with you, dear students, about the SparkNote-ization of reading, which trains you to believe that we read merely to collect facts and that story is merely about plot. The literary critic Christopher Clausen has said that all of literature attempts to answer, either directly or indirectly, two questions: 1. What kind of world is this? And 2. How shall we live in it? The Common Core's two questions? 1. What does it say in line 7 about carbon emissions (or some other topic not related to literature), and 2. How many points will my grade go down if I can't come up with a counter-argument incorporating line 2?

The very first sample ELA Regents provided by New York State presented nine passages for the students to analyze. Only two of the samples provided were literary (one poem and one prose excerpt). If you recall, the last two recent Regents exams, thankfully, provided a bit of respite from scientific texts and legal documents, with the inclusion of a story excerpt and a writing question about a literary device. The major essay itself, however, is still almost identical to the Social Studies DBQ (document-based question), where you construct an argument based on articles unrelated to literature.

What does this mean for you guys? In the short term, consider that last year, College Board exec Trevor Packer tweeted, "I am sorry to report that the AP Literature exam scores this year are the lowest they have been in decades." Now, you know I'm skeptical when it comes to tests, and the sole purpose of AP Lit is not merely test prep; it's to provide you with a college-level education. But the AP Lit test is a *good test*. Something is not working. More concerning than test results are the long-term consequences for you all. A curriculum based primarily on the mechanics of reading for facts takes away the very element that makes stories worthwhile: there's no curiosity, nor any lessons urging humans to consider how to live, interact, achieve our aspirations, use language carefully, listen closely and with humility, or deal with suffering.

Please understand that the less we emphasize the humanities as a culture, the more shocking become the eruptions of bullying and violence in what has become a national epidemic. In the era of this new normal, the battle cry for uniformity has necessitated the concrete as the common denominator. To go beyond that would be to create discrepancies among different classes. We can't have anybody comparing classes! We need to protect ourselves by all doing the same thing! Variety? Monstrous. No time for creative assignments. Poetry? Forget it.

We have prioritized research, argument, and "deliverables" (yes, "deliverable" has become a noun) over esoteric, epic, lyrical thinking. Is it any surprise that when we take away literature, which teaches children empathy, compassion, and imagination, we must then replace it with anti-bullying assemblies and metal detectors? We can't complain about the younger generation's lack of interpersonal and critical skills when it is we who strip you of wonder, when we banish the guiding premises that help you all reflect, connect, and become socially mature.

Making a claim and defending it with several artifacts is a valid undertaking and a valuable life skill. In its current iteration, however, the problem with the Regents format is its over-representation. Nudging aside writing to learn, embracing the complexities of story, and listening closely to a poet or novelist's message, its dense saturation in the curriculum has lead to some troubling habits of mind.

Increasingly, I have noticed that many of you are more befuddled than ever during writing sessions or discussions exploring a topic in literature: you want to know what we think? Just tell us what the answer is. What's the formula for the essay? Is this sentence good? What do you want me to write? I will give you what you want. You become so concerned about the "right" answer that you don't have time to enjoy the process of exercising your own judgment confidently.

And why wouldn't you and your families be concerned? There are so many demands on your time: SATs, PSATs, ACTs, college admissions, school tests, sports, activities, and homework. We know that student tension and depression have escalated to alarming heights. With over-packed schedules and the emphasis on the "right" transcript, college, career, awards, number of AP classes, and text interpretation, it's no wonder that so many of you sit anxiously in class, stymied, pens poised over your desks, unable to commit to placing words on paper.

Because in your world of exams, résumé-building, high stakes scores, and academic rankings, you might be...*wrong*. Such timidity shuts down conversations and makes you over-reliant on a number grade as the barometer of your personal worth. Take heart, dear students! You're not fragile. You're resilient intellectual warriors! In and out of the classroom, our Draconian focus on uniformity—of argument structure, pedagogy, and our own teaching philosophies—belies the goal of you the students finding your own voice.

Yet writing accomplishes that very goal. It doesn't merely record what's already all figured out mentally. It helps you discover what you think in the first place. Personally, I don't want to teach you what to think. I want to teach you *how* to think. And if we are doing that the right way, well then, wouldn't high Regents scores be a natural side-effect of real learning? As opposed to its *telos*?

Many of you freeze when you are asked what you think, and it's not because you're all lazy slobs or cellphone-zombie burnouts. Mostly, you have a genuine desire to do well in something that simply provides no joy. Just so you know, young, enthusiastic educators new to teaching often feel the same way. They are so eager to please, but feel stuck: their students must pass these exams. They must stick to the format!

To the most well-meaning of teachers and students, finding a voice and thinking critically are luxuries that a test-driven curriculum just cannot afford. We cannot compress learning into two dimensions and then complain that student work lacks depth.

Our emphasis on the article-based argumentative essay (claim, concession, evidence) has edged out close reading and interpretation of dense, rich literary passages. With the over-saturation of one type of essay, meaning gets boiled down to a yes-no-maybe answer devoid of nuance. Well-intentioned educators who may rejoice, "Now students can't argue about what a book means!" run the risk, not only of discouraging their students from speaking freely, but also of extinguishing those ineffable moments in a classroom that make your minds come alive.

The Common Core is indeed common, but in all the wrong ways. The curriculum gets boiled down to concrete information gleaned from the basics of reading short articles for information. Of course data assists our instruction. Of course we need to be forever searching for meaningful methods that work. Do not suppose that I am suggesting that finding answers is merely a matter of frolicking in fields barefoot while making daisy chains and braiding each others' hair. After all, a text does not always mean what we want it to mean.

Education should prepare you for the fact that, to life's most important questions, there are *many* right answers, just as any life problems call for multiple approaches and remedies. None of them are simple. English should be celebrated for emphasizing "thinking outside of the box", not just checking off the right one. Throughout your lives, you'll have to write for all kinds of purposes, beyond the DBQ or research paper (more on that later). Trust me, you don't want to learn just a couple of writing formats or strategies of observation. In your professional and personal future, you'll have to vary your tone to suit your audience. Life will throw you all kinds of challenges, and they won't all come from one direction. Maybe your solutions shouldn't either.

The pressure for uniformity has the potential to create tension among incredibly talented, passionate teachers who just want to do the right thing. The new method almost generates watchfulness; the call is for compliance, even obedience—not excellence.

Recent research provides intriguing ideas about offering students choices in what they read. I've talked with you about this, dear students, and I know how exciting this prospect is for you. Enthusiasm and engagement tend to skyrocket when you each own your literacy, taking charge of your identity as a reader. How liberating! Breathe in the exhilaration. Proud of overseeing your own growth, you feel empowered and inspired.

Shouldn't it be the same with your teachers?

Aren't your classes better when your teacher presents books…that she loves? We are lucky when teaching provides the luxury of letting educators create lessons that work well for you based on what we love and what you need. Now consider the teacher who must adhere to new strictures the state has provided, or align her reading lists with another department's content. As hard as she tries to find and muster enthusiasm for literary texts about PACs or congressional districting, imagine her difficulty in guiding you all through that curriculum and hoping to inspire you with a love of reading.

It's unlikely that those classrooms would then prepare students for the independence of the choice-driven college experience or career, or vibrate with that spark of magic that reaches into the eternal when professors are given more autonomy. At the university level, Humanities courses need not exist to justify one another, because the community implicitly accepts that each subject is inherently valuable, celebrating the diversity of content and pedagogy that a well-rounded education necessitates.

College professors are responsible for providing challenging reading and writing instruction, but whether it's a 101 course, remediation class, or Toni Morrison seminar, I imagine (maybe too naïvely) that they are allotted more freedom to incorporate texts and methods that best suit their students. Their seminars about a particular author, genre, literary movement, or topic will crackle with infectious purpose and joy.

An English teacher with a master's thesis in Romanticism may have inspired students in the past with his specialized passion for a wild-eyed, disheveled Byron, but now he must curb his fervor to stay lockstep with what someone else (the state) has decided. After all, his colleague whose thesis was on modern American poetry does the same. Vanishing is the mining of language for its perplexing subtleties and connotations, gone the way of an educator's sense of voice and the freedom to apply professional discretion to discover what works.

Rather than one prescriptive reading list at each level—a rigid set of six books that every student must read (which creates all sorts of problems with book rotations anyway)—let's reinvigorate the selection with fresher titles. Reframe each grade-level book list as book *banks* that offer more diverse options and offer a rich well of literature. Broaden the pool of books available for each grade, enriching the selection with liveliness and variety. Try literature circles. Teachers can decide that year's titles based on the unique tastes and skills of that year's students, current events, and their own level of enthusiasm. Providing this autonomy is no easy proposition philosophically or financially; it requires both trust in the teachers' expertise and open pockets. Let good teachers choose. Instant climate change.

If we want more student engagement at the high school level, try giving every public school English teacher a blank slate and a budget. Tell them each to pick one book they would love to teach. Order the books and let them have at it. Watch them relish the process of sinking their teeth into what they have chosen, just as you students will when you are given a voice and a choice. Honor teachers' professionalism by giving them room to share that joy with their students.

We want to follow our instincts toward growth, not curb them based on the lowest common denominator, which then becomes a ceiling. At the local level, this is not any individual's fault. It's the system. We want to share with you and with each other what we love most about our subject, and keep learning ourselves. How frustrating for teachers and those who guide them, doing their best to lead in these times.

Professional development for teachers has usually been pedagogically-based, but why isn't it related to our specific subject? As teachers, we stagnate when we stop learning about our areas of interest. How wonderful, to deepen our knowledge about a particular writer, genre, or literary movement. Offer us courses in, say, Magical Realism, the Beat Generation, Korean poetry, Dorothy Parker, Irish drama, *Gulliver's Travels*, James Baldwin, or post-colonial Haitian literature.

Many teachers are so thirsty for more literature and writing that we've taken advanced degrees and post-graduate courses in our content area on our own time; we know we aren't likely to get the chance in a public school setting. Our workshops discuss writing, but we never actually get to do any writing or try out new strategies ourselves. Teachers are longing for updated professional development that refuels our knowledge and passion in our beloved subject. The best PD I've ever experienced was led by a college writing professor. Feed us, we beg of you!

Instead of weathering the storm by taking cover under the one way of doing things, let's be a little more daring. Let's try new methods to keep up with your changing world. Educators desperately want to inspire you to go beyond the bare minimum of thought and expression to become articulate, mindful individuals. We shouldn't give up on expecting you to enjoy reading, nor should we dissuade you from exploring ideas to which there isn't one concrete answer.

Should schools maintain a high level of rigor? Absolutely. And if I can ever strike the perfect balance of rigor without panic, you'll be the first to know. Yet we need a curriculum created by teachers and communities who love their content and the classroom, not one handed down to us from a decentralized committee of experts whose mandates materialize in labyrinthine, tortured edu-speak.

The Common Core worships at the altar of "all on the same page," but teachers never had a say in what book that page should come from. We need to respect the benchmarks reminding us what you need to learn at each level, but we should celebrate that there are so many effective ways of getting there. Using data to innovate student learning need not require a love affair with lock-step synchronization.

There's often a growing sense of indignation when people lament the Common Core. Understand that I don't tell you any of this to stoke outrage. I tell you so that you may sidestep speedbumps that have such a momentary showing in time, and open yourselves up to your own path to knowledge, one that isn't bound by temporality or fickle trends.

When I first started teaching, public education was still reeling from the open classroom movement and was about to delve into No Child Left Behind. In between, I remember hours and hours of reworking what we were supposed to, and every alteration was supposed to be the penultimate antidote for what ails public education.

There was the phase where students couldn't earn lower than a 50% on any single assignment, even if the student didn't turn it in. Next, a student's average wasn't based on numbers, but on letters, each with their own system: students who got an A in the first quarter, then didn't turn in a thing past October, would still pass the course with a C. Another era dictated that every assignment must have two dates: a due date and a deadline. I'd explain that one more, but it would require both a PowerPoint and a desire to fathom the difference.

I'd feel differently had the modifications been locally generated, with input from our administrators, colleagues, and community. Each reform I've mentioned, however, was prescribed by a faceless committee well-versed in theories. And each one had me frazzled and scrambling around to make changes I didn't always condone or understand.

Public education has always depended, like a sad and simpering Blanche DuBois, on the kindness of strangers. Don't let it trouble you. I will tell you how it will go: the next gentleman caller (a.k.a. tech tycoon) who wants to make a healthy donation to public schools will get to decide how it must be spent. After all, he went to school, so he is clearly an expert about how school should go. Then teachers get escorted offstage to professional development in straitjackets and hope that you, our students, don't get burned by the bare light bulb of reality.

You may recall Hamlet's disgust when his mother, with good intentions, tries to console her son about the loss of his beloved father by telling him that death is a common experience. Hamlet, repulsed by his mother's hasty remarriage to his uncle, slyly casts his mother as low-brow when he disdainfully agrees, "Aye, madam, 'tis common." If you understood the allusion to *Hamlet* in the title of this chapter, or if anything in the last paragraph gave you the urge to yell, "*STELLAAAAAAAA*!", then thank your wealth of knowledge about stories and literature. You can communicate in metaphor.

To speak the transcendent language of story, even in a passing allusion, is to be linked, even briefly, to a mythical world shared and understood by others in one shining, communal moment. You may nod and connect Hamlet's wry retort with the universals we each encounter in our lifespan. When similar occasions in your lives call for the phrase, you already have the vocabulary for how to process and frame your experience. This is what education does. It gives you context and guides you toward the wellspring of meaning.

These days, when I hear rumblings about new reforms coming our way in a couple of years, well, yawn. I'm not going to get upset about it right now, and neither should you. Theories change too frequently to see each new trend as a permanent catastrophe. This current iteration isn't there yet.

Thankfully, we keep talking about how to advance education, understanding that there's no panacea for something so imperative and protean. Whatever comes next, don't worry. We'll learn something afresh, try new strategies, and embrace the ones that work, because many actually do. What you can do is focus on the well of knowledge that irrigates your darkest corners. Find and apply the eternal things that matter to you, intrigue you, and connect you with the world.

As ever,

Ms. Gavin

Real Talk

Ms. Gavin: Okay, clear off your desks. Reading quiz.

Student: UUGHHMPPH! Of COURSE! The ONE NIGHT I didn't read!

Friend: You said that yesterday.

Student: (*Mutters and complains throughout quiz. Tries to look around for support in rebelling, but nobody's on board. Shields eyes with hand on forehead, tries to read neighbor's paper, can't see the writing. Becomes more enraged.*) Is this a JOKE? How're we seriously supposed to know all of this and know the deeper meaning? We have to UNDERSTAND what we READ?!

We have to know QUOTES?! Are we seriously expected to remember the characters and details from the book?!

Ms. Gavin: Yes.

Writing: Getting Bitter Before Getting Better

Dear Students,

In eighth grade, I earned a 73 on every essay I wrote in English class. Every single one. I just didn't get it. This girl loved reading. I read so much it got in the way of school-work, and I wanted to be a writer when I grew up. 73? I didn't understand.

That was the problem. It wasn't the grade that discouraged me; it was not understanding why. My teacher underlined and circled a lot on my papers, and sometimes there were abbreviations I didn't understand. What was "quote inc."? "BW"? Squiggly line?

I had no idea. I had always done well in English, because I had always loved reading and writing. Maybe also because I smiled a lot (a nervous habit that probably made me come off a little freaky). But when we moved to a different part of the country, I realized that while enthusiasm was a good start, I had much to learn.

I hadn't ever had to make friends; I had so many that I'd just grown up with, taking for granted the connection that our shared childhood fortified. I hadn't once in my life walked through a school hallway knowing nobody, nor had I ever stayed home alone. I'd never had a locker or multiple classes in one day. What I did have was a southern twang and a mullet, and I lost a spelling bee because I didn't understand the Boston accent. Lizzid? Oh, *lizard*.

And then I wasn't even doing well in English. English was supposed to be my jam! Not that this is something I'm proud of now, but at the time, I just shut down instead of trying to get better. The technicalities were just so boring, I grumbled. I told myself the lie that we have all told ourselves at some point: that writing is all just subjective anyway. Deep down, we know it's really not—there is, unfortunately, such a thing as bad writing. Whether it's the ease of reading clear writing, or the torture of working through convoluted, labored sentences, we've all read both sorts. We welcome one and spurn the other, and can easily spot the difference.

I still struggle with writing, and cringe over sentences I wrote five years ago, last week, this morning. Sometimes I wonder why I do this to myself. I can guarantee you that this very book you are holding is a source of embarrassment because of all its imperfections that are now glaring to me. I am flinching at the thought of having to read this uneven chapter again and at the ongoing circumstance of its being out there, anywhere.

I want you to understand that there's no "there" there. Writing is vexing because, whether or not you love to read, it often feels worse to fail an essay than a math test. You've heard that writing is a process, and I'm here to tell you that it's a craft you keep honing throughout your lives. A low writing grade right now should not urge you to think poorly of yourself or writing. You leave that to me. (Just kidding.) It just means that we have work to do, and that you will edge ever closer to clear expression.

After reading your writing, I know just where we need to go. Believe that there are concrete strategies you will learn to get better and better. Be open to hearing what they are. There are so many moving components that make us feel in over our head at times—grammar, diction, structure, analysis, voice. You keep at it. Keep practicing, logging every word on your sentence odometer and running up the mileage on your writing life.

Will there ever be a finished whole in all its shining, perfect unity? A point at which you as a writer perch triumphantly upon the peak of writing mastery? I don't know; you'd have to ask one of the great writers who have trod upon this earth. From where I stand, the answer is no, and that answer isn't anything that should worry you in the least. Writing is complex, and so are you. We'll always feel thwarted by the abyss between what we say and what we mean. Writing practice helps us get closer and closer to the truth, and the closer we get, the more we are satisfied about thinking and communicating clearly.

In eighth grade I was the caricature of what *not* to do to advance one's writing. Getting essays back took on its own routine. My English notebook had a pocket of shame in the very back where I shoved all my mediocre essays, hoping to hide my work. I told my embarrassed self that I was shielding it from others' sight, but, really, I was trying to hide it from my own. Instead of focusing on the teacher's comments, I'd sneak glances at the papers of classmates to find out what they got. Spotting a 94, I'd look away sheepishly. (You're no help! I need a complaining ally!) It never occurred to me to ask them how they did so well, or what their thought process was.

Longing to please the teacher, I was far too shy and self-conscious ever to go over any of my writing with her. Blunders in my awkward bearing and clumsy writing irritated her, I assumed. I never thought she saw me or knew how much I cared about English. That responsibility, I realized, too late, was up to me.

So I'd go home and read everything *but* what was assigned. No matter what I told myself at the time, *I* was the one who allowed myself to become disconnected from sixth period English. Reading class was another story altogether; that was taught by one of my two favorite middle school teachers of all time (Ms. Capone and Mrs. Paull, I love you!). Understand that there was never any hostility in English class whatsoever; I just gradually internalized my presence as a vague irrelevance. Success was fully in my own power, but I had yet to realize it. I can't change that now, but I can help you avoid the pitfalls that held me back.

Dear students, if you are upset about your grade, I know just how you feel. You might feel as if your entire being is being called into question. Maybe you are tormented by that pit in your stomach, or your face gets hot and you can hear your heart pounding in your ears. Before you go to the bathroom and call your mom in tears, hang on. Here is what to do when you get a low writing grade:

1. Roll your eyes and stomp in outrage. Leave the classroom in a huff at the end of the period. It's okay. Now, the next step is a topic for debate, because you may have the urge to crumple up your paper and throw it in the garbage on the way out as a dramatic gesture. Trust me that this won't help you become a better writer, only embarrass you later.

2. Mentally curse me, my incompetence, and the assignment. Be like Grendel and flip off the sky. Best if not done in public.

3. Go home and scream into a pillow, drowning in rage as you gaze into the abyss of this grade. Writing feels personal. Investment is good.

4. Change into sweatpants. Eat your favorite food and stay off your phone.

5. Detach yourself from your emotions, particularly the mindset that your essay is way better than the points you earned. Even if it feels like pretending, don a cloak of humility, since learning takes listening. Refocus your investment on determining to improve. Just try it.

6. Watch *The Office* and old Bugs Bunny shows. There's a particular clip I recommend, but don't watch the whole episode. It's the one where Bugs Bunny, to evade the hunter Elmer Fudd, pretends to be a barber and gives

him a make-over to the score of Rossini's *The Barber of Seville*. First of all, that's a great technique of eluding enemies that frankly just never occurred to me. And there's something therapeutic about watching Bugs Bunny massage Elmer's bald head and create a fruit salad on top of it.

7. When you are in a calmer state of mind, re-read my comments and feedback on your paper. Breathe deeply as you go over the sheet of mini-lessons I create from your essays (see Appendix D), including the student samples.

8. Come see me when you've had a catharsis and exorcised the strong emotions. When you can detach yourself from the grade and your despair has gone from boiling, to tepid, to room temperature, let's talk. If you truly don't know where you went astray, or don't see how your paper differs from the exemplars, come on in and we'll go over it with a fresh perspective.

No educator is angry when students really try; there's no hostility here. Helping is what we do. I promise you that writing conferences aren't about interrogation or chastising. The more open to feedback you are, the more your writing will improve. My goal is to make you a better writer, and that means giving you an honest assessment of where your writing truly is. False praise would only set you up for failure later on.

Some of you want teachers to be your friend or therapist. I'd have no wish to, and neither would you, not really. Why do I want you to reread that last sentence? Because that is not what you need from me or anything I am qualified to provide. Please hear me. I'm not that person.

Yet this information shouldn't make you underestimate my complete buy-in when it comes to your well-being. I don't want you to be sitting in a college classroom or board meeting someday, feeling totally outclassed by the skills of those around you. I want you to be the one intimidating and impressing other students, just because you're *that good*.

Sincerely,

Ms. Gavin

Movie Teachers

It starts with hearing about the notorious class:
Good luck with *those* students, they warn her.
At first the miracles are small.
The worst kid agrees to sit down.
The second worst takes out a pencil.
Then they're all showing her how to dance.

By the end of the first half hour she has them eagerly atten-
tive
and they're rapping their feelings
and she's defending them from other teachers who are cynical and condescending
and who wear orthopedic shoes.
She visits their houses, gets them jobs, bribes their parents.
She works three jobs because that's what people who care do.
She's saving them from the gang leader, holding their hands
in rehab,
diving in front of them in street fights, healing their leprosy.

DEAR STUDENTS

Her desk is always clean.

At her school the classes are four minutes:
class starts, she tells a few jokes, and
at least two students cry because they are so moved.
Perhaps there's time for a hip-hop chorus line.
The closing bell rings, and not a student stirs.

They're always reading poems. No novels.
They write her a song at the end of the year and present it to
the cruel superintendent who resents her innovation.
They never want to know their average
because there's no grading to be done.

She and her seventh period solve the energy crisis.
Her first period establishes diplomatic relations that disarm
North Korea.
No time for nouns.
She feeds them inspiration and gets them to lap up moon-
beams
that come out of their ears.
They sprout wings from their formerly hunched shoulder
blades.
In the final scene her students carry her around the town
square on their shoulders, cheering,
and she becomes so luminous that she dissolves into a blind-
ing
light and ascends to another realm,
leaving behind a sobbing crowd chanting her name.

Scene. Lights up. Progress reports are due.

Losing Legends in the Details:
Darth Vader and Writer's Block

Teacher has been staring at a blank screen for ten minutes. She cannot let her students down. She must write. She opens the web browser and sees about buying the next book in the Poldark *series. Four hours later, she has taken her dog Lolly for a walk. Her kitchen floor gleams like the day it was installed. She has cleaned out the attic and figured out a shortcut to nuclear fission. There is still nothing on the screen in front of her.*

* * *

Dear Students,

There is one question that frequently comes up in class: can creative writing really be taught? Let me back up.

To escape the writing desert that had left my inspiration parched, I attended a creative writing workshop in Manhattan a few years ago. It was pretty dismal. Maybe as an English teacher I just get tired of going over the definitions of plot and point of view. I'm impatient. I just want to start writing, because discipline is the hardest part of writing for me. When it comes to feeling frozen in the face of committing words to paper and running the risk of killing an idea, I know what you each go through. Now I revisit the question, can one really teach creative writing?

Several years after undergrad, I was living in Boston and working, first at a daycare center and a nightclub, and then at a publishing house doing data entry. Heeding the call to write, I matriculated in a prestigious MFA program in Creative Writing. I sold my car and listened to the *Flashdance* theme on Amtrak all the way down to Penn Station, frightening seatmates with my vigorous fist pumps. Because this was **it**. This was what my life was going to be. I had arrived!

I hadn't arrived. It was all wrong from day one.

Even though MFA programs have helped to shape countless writers, I knew in my core that it was the wrong time and place for me. Removed from the outside world with our cushion of student loans and lofty ideals of artistic purity, we didn't actually do any writing. Maybe writing requires self-indulgence, in that it involves a lot of navel gazing and groping feebly around for ways to say just what you mean. But instead of writing life by living life, we all seemed united in our self-congratulatory echo chamber, one that resonated with disdain for others' earnest attempts.

I felt like I had to stick with it—I mean, who drops out of a program this competitive? How embarrassing. What would I do with my life now? Those of you who have gone through the college application or transfer process know what I mean here. Yet I feared that if I stayed, my success would be dependent eternally on the sanction of others, particularly those who rode the condescending euphoria of labeling everybody else as poseurs.

So I did the obvious thing. I quit the program and moved down to the Gulf Shores of Alabama, where I worked at The Olive Garden. (I mean, how cliché!)

It would actually be several more years (after working at a radio station, a medical supply company, an alternative newspaper, a bookstore, and a temp agency) before I gave in to the calling of my life, one I had been fleeing for so long because I had prized some pretty silly visions of what success looked and felt like.

Don't feel like you must follow a set trajectory in your lives, dear students. Unhappy in a major or in a job? Things don't go as you planned? That's normal. Move on. Just please, whatever you do, *don't ever take time off employment to "find yourself."* Contribute to society by joining the workforce; it doesn't have to be a career. Find yourself by working, questioning, and seeking. Your road will meander and fork in inexplicable ways. The universe will bonk you on the head repeatedly with clear messages until you see.

The urge to write never left me, so a while back I thought an eminent day-long writers' workshop would be just the thing. As it turned out, just as I did with the MFA program so many years earlier, I did the Irish goodbye before it was over, wishing for either a time machine or a refund.

So let's revisit the question. Can creative writing be taught?

The workshop opened with a lecture about characterization and why it's important, but the instructor's anecdotes seemed to be givens. For every hour the teacher spoke, she gave us ten minutes of writing. She would ask students here and there to recite their work, then re-read it out loud line by line so she could dissect how each phrase could be better.

At one point the teacher mockingly narrated a passage from a romance novel. Egged on by guffaws, she became more acerbic, sarcastically reciting other passages from popular bestsellers. True, there was a lot of "telling" in the excerpts, and the texts may not all have been heavyweights of the western canon. But here's a truth for you. It's *really hard* to write readable books that make people eager to turn the page.

It's too easy to sneer at something and get cheap laughs from students who are desperately eager to please. I'm not sure such pointed criticism, particularly when strangers in a large class then must share their own work, sets the right tone. Its derision just puts people on edge. Plus, let's be real: aren't we a little wary of writers who mock Dan Brown, because, for all the stylistic faults they swear are obvious, don't those writers secretly wish they *were* Dan Brown?

The instructor mocked other popular authors, then moved on to criticize an even easier target: the American President, with all the usual tropes, a most unwelcome intrusion in the middle of a writing class about making meaning. Sardonic wisecracks about a political leader's ineptitude? Now there's something we've never heard before.

Her aside, however, made me think of *Star Wars*, an epic that reaches back into our collective unconscious and speaks to us in a meaningful way.[1] She gave the usual advice about writing, such as, "Show, don't tell." You've seen this comment on your papers plenty of times. Yet if a story is all about showing, one has an extremely long novel that is not particularly interesting to read. If we were to re-write *Star Wars* with the workshop's advice, the storm troopers would be worried drones anxious about feeding their families, and we would have the details about how it feels to be inside that stifling, sweat-sticky storm trooper uniform. That in itself has potential to be intriguing, but it's the opening to another type of story altogether. Saving the galaxy? We'd never even make it through the character's morning bath.

The instructor recited an excerpt, with hushed reverence, from a modern novel—beautifully written, but in the end, it was a multi-page description of the inside of somebody's mouth. Then another passage, this time providing painstaking details about an unremarkable file cabinet. Unlike the first round of readings, however, this time the students all nodded sagely. *This* was what we were all to aim for, eliminating all traces of telling in any form. But is this method of showing the only way to write fiction well? Do linguistic calisthenics about a file cabinet, unrelated to anything else in the story, make us wonder about what it means to be human? Maybe so. Maybe not. What happens when verbose details and attempts at being avant-garde become ends in

---

[1] You, dear students, have joked that no one knows exactly what makes Darth Vader and the Death Star evil. Why are they evil? We are merely *told* they are in the beginning, and we don't have much beyond the black cloak and Vader's menacing ventilator to back that up. Opponents say that, you know, blowing up an entire planet for fun tiptoes on that gray line of ethics... These are great homeroom conversations. In any case, Darth Vader is evil. We must accept that for the premise of the story.

themselves? Sometimes we actually need telling so that we may reach the universal. We never know, for example, what Elizabeth Bennet looks like. Do we need to?

While our priority on showing over telling is the current trend in writing, strict adherence to it can trick us into creating works that aren't grounded in meaning, blurring the distinction between showing and showing off. Placing too much value on these *tours de force* may be discouraging true literary communities. That day I rode home on the Metro-North reminding myself it was just one workshop; not all writing programs were like this. If they were, they'd all produce cohorts of delusional hopefuls fraught with sycophantic neuroses.

To bring truly great stories back to the forefront of our imaginations, we want to think about why language is significant and how storytelling gives meaning to our lives. We must feel Frodo's failure on the cliff of Mount Doom but needn't hear how his hair looks, where he goes to the bathroom in the woods, or how sore his feet are. His *hamartia* echoes our own in ways we can't explain, but do understand, on a primal level. We need to follow Don Quijote, becoming amused, appalled, and inspired by his often-misguided exploits, our own heroic impulses fueled by his cinematic imagination. We don't need to know what he had for breakfast.

So maybe the writing workshop helped after all, because here I am and here we have a new musing and hopefully it will be a good musing. A little Gertrude Stein polysyndeton for you there. (That's for you, period four.)

My favorite English teacher in high school (Hi, Mr. Schauble!) introduced us to Christopher Clausen's concept that I've mentioned before: that all great literature attempts to answer, either directly or indirectly, two questions. What kind of world is this, and how do we live in it? These queries have been replaced in modern pop culture with the questions, "Who am I, and how can I market that identity?"

Perhaps we have taken the Delphic aphorism "Know thyself" to feverish pitches and lost our way. We may not be looking *within*, but we can barely tear our gazes away from own brand. Many of us have become addicted to the image we want others to have of us, ever cranking out highly curated likenesses in a feverish attempt to garner, at best, approval. At worst, envy.

These narratives show a lot, but don't tell. And limiting ourselves to showing has led to a habit of selfie-gazing that has hardly brought us any closer to fulfillment. Prefigured by my former aspirants in the MFA program, we turn over our sense of individual worth, crushingly, to the cursory estimation of others. We gaze at and primp ourselves with such virtuosity that many no longer seek knowledge about what is outside of us, wonder about magnitude, or dream about the ways in which we are all connected.

It turns out that writing itself is the best teacher of writing. Maybe we can't teach creative writing, but creative writing certainly has a lot to teach *us.*

Best regards,

Ms. Gavin

It's Late, Not a Tsunami

(*Early spring in room S112. Today an essay is due. Student rushes into class with no paper and wearing tragedy-face. There has been no real family emergency preventing her from doing the assignment. Out of breath, with an air of angst and despair, she rushes up to the teacher, who is about to start class.*)

Student:	Can I talk to you?
Ms. Gavin:	Maybe after class?
Student:	Well, it's just that—like, I know that I—
Ms. Gavin:	Just turn it in tomorrow.
Friend:	(*Whispering furiously. He has been through this himself and wants to help.*) Bro, bro, bro. The rest of us got the work done. She's *not* going to want to hear the story! Take the fall. Do it! Do it now!

Student: Shh! Don't call me "bro," you sexist. I got this. (*Still thinking that a panicked story showing overly dramatic concern will solve this and garner sympathy.*) It's not an excuse. It's just that I had my other notebook and the earthquake and the project and the printer and the puking and the practice and the thing—

Ms. Gavin: I don't want to hear the story. I get it. Turn it in tomorrow.

Student: It's just that—I mean—I was really tired—my mom will e-mail you—

Other student: (*Tries not to laugh but fails.*) Your MOM? You're *seventeen*. (*Students titter and guffaw. Kid in back row wails, "Mommeeee!"*)

Student: But the thing is, with the lawnmower and the jelly sandwich and the dog and the rock-climbing and the papercut and the computer—

Friend: (*Head in hands.*) Bro! I *told* you!

Ms. Gavin: (*Hand up, with a detached smile.*)
Way too much emotional
investment and time for me. You
don't have it for whatever
reason. Turn it in tomorrow and
accept the late points. I have no
consolation for you. I cannot
give you the comfort you seek
for not having your work done.
Class, take out your books.

Friend: Crash and burn, Mav. Crash and
burn.

Boccaccio, McCarthy,
and the Compassion Cure

Dear Students,

What if a ship of corpses drifted into a major harbor downtown, and within months, fifty percent of the continent's population died? Asking for a friend.

Giovanni Boccaccio's *Decameron* is a vivid eyewitness account of the terrible plague that swept through Europe starting in 1347, when a dozen infected ships showed up in the port of Messina. By some accounts, the Black Death killed one of every three people, more in urban areas. According to Boccaccio, the worst horror isn't actually the agony and gruesome deaths suffered by the victims (descriptions of whose symptoms are horrific), nor is it the superstitions embraced by villagers: it's the loss of human compassion.

We understand this in the millennium, with its pangs of unkindness both miniscule and appalling; just look at footage of Black Friday shoppers trampling each other. Cormac McCarthy feels it too. The post-apocalyptic world endured by the surviving father and son in his novel *The Road* also witnesses the demolition of mercy. Rousseau's natural man, unlike Hobbes' human monster, lives for himself, but it is pity that holds him back from hurting other people. In McCarthy's post-apocalyptic *katabasis*, however, the world has fallen way too far for such naïve notions. Empathy is our last remaining mouse squeak of humanity.

Like the figurative "fire" the father desperately tries to keep alive for his son, all signifiers of pity have been reduced to ashes around them. We may lose our things in all their very trappings of thingness, and with loss of life may go our scraps of shared stories and traditions. But the fire dies when we lose the element of charity and stop caring for one another.

The ultimate, most chilling image Boccaccio evokes is the example of women who have abandoned their children, just as the suicidal mother does in *The Road*, lighting up discussion boards with incendiary controversy. In the monstrous cannibals, McCarthy presents a different kind of plague with the same side effect: the raw and primal need to survive for the self alone.

Whenever we wonder if *The Road* is tragedy, you all identify Aristotle's pity and fear very well, but then remember that the novel doesn't end with a character's fall from grace. In fact, the father's ideals may be challenged throughout the journey, but he dies an uncompromised man in that which matters the most: he has kept the fire alive for his son, who will now possess a memory, in a memoryless world, of what love truly is. The fire burns incandescently and eternally. You are initially puzzled, dear students, when I posit that, in literature, death is not the worst thing that can happen to a character. Were *The Road*'s father, like the crazed Don Quijote, to renounce his previous life maxims about not feeding on others, the devastation would be total.

The survivors in *The Decameron* regain their humanity by retreating from the sickened city, seeking refuge at a remote villa in an Edenic, pastoral setting. Here they purify themselves both physically and emotionally, cleaning off the filth of callous disregard for others and purging the monomaniacal demands of self-preservation. I hope you each have a sacred psychological or physical space where you can do the same. Each character in *The Decameron* must tell tales, reviving the fire of connection by drinking the elixir of storytelling. In sharing and absorbing narrative, they regain the ability to imagine what others are going through—and everybody is going through something.

When love and empathy face extinction, only storytelling is mighty enough to bring us back from the abyss of savagery. It *has* to be stories. They're the epic heroes who attune us to the joys and sorrows of others and redirect our self-absorbed gazes outward. Their healing waters re-establish damaged human bonds by cultivating awe, laughter, and empathy.

What does this mean for you? For starters, let's be real about your community service hours. Suppose that, instead of "volunteering in your uncle's office," you had to spend the last two weeks of every school year out in the wilderness with a guide and no technology. You'd reconnect with the natural world, each other, and your deepest self. Some of you would hate it, but would learn what it's like to be fully in the world instead of swiping a screen. Imagine learning about life by existing wholly *in* it, free from that twitchy urge to check your phone. That steam-train of images and icons charging around your brain would slow down and ultimately fall silent. You'd have the best conversations of your lives.

Your annual tech detox would provide you all with an experience so raw and pure that it just couldn't be replaced by any kind of virtual simulation. What would happen if you and your peers weren't subjects to your screens, if you felt the satisfaction of a meal well-earned, if you grew to accept and even welcome the restorative powers of silence? Quietude wouldn't terrify you; you'd feel no urge to stifle your true self or craft an exterior façade to shield yourself from the world. You'd emerge as more grounded, focused, compassionate individuals. Watch what happens. Witness your society healing.

"Okay, okay, we got it. Be nice." But when it comes to mindful compassion, *do* we get it, really? Our very souls depend on an honest answer. You know that younger kids have dutifully listened to what we have told them about bullying, a word they encounter so often it has almost lost its meaning. From a young age, children can parrot what they've heard. The stories they write often feature a person so bullied that, invariably, he's driven to harm either himself out of despondency, or others out of revenge. Sometimes the narrative goes the other way, ending with someone speaking up for the harassed, or the outcast getting invited to the lunch table and welcomed seamlessly into the fold. Not a bad start, but it just shouldn't be the end.

Our cultural contagion is the spreading inability to feel for one another. *With* one another. A life without connection eats away at the core of our being. If you, dear students, are only hearing, "Be nice or you'll create a killer," then we have garbled the message for you. We've turned compassion into a show of niceness for self-preservation as opposed to a lesson about truly imagining how another person feels. Kindness doesn't mean we tiptoe around disturbed individuals so they won't harm us.

Yet it's inevitable that outbreaks of violence are all-too-frequent reminders of what can happen when an individual's pity lies unburnished. How can we *not* talk about it? Maybe there are days when you're apprehensive about coming to school, or maybe you just don't understand how human beings can be so despicable. You're not alone in this, and there's no easy answer to the problem of why people inflict such suffering on one another. But please know that the stories we tell and absorb as a culture don't just express who we are: they *shape* who we are. The images we expose children to are nothing short of an all-out assault on their psyches. There is absolutely no way compassion can withstand a barrage of nihilistic narratives and addictive images of senseless, repeated brutality.

We might wonder whether violent perpetrators were ever able to feel anything kind for others. Before their humanity died, before they thought to take refuge in a glowing screen of not-life, before their empathy atrophied, could there ever have been a point at which they could have connected to someone, anyone, in a real way?

Might they have found a kindred spirit or two (like L .M. Montgomery's Anne Shirley and Diana Barry), whose very friendship would have attested to the universal human onuses of suffering, alienation, anger, and a pervasive feeling of being lost? Because kindred spirits also bear witness to the unfathomable joys of connection. They stoke the courageous yearning to become fully known and to experience completely somebody else's life.

Sometime around late elementary school, the innocent sameness we all shared at the bus-stop began to separate itself out in disparities we came to see through traumatic or disquieting lessons. We learned that a selfless friend doesn't air your private woes just to stay relevant and be the one lording information authoritatively. They'll never indicate exclusivity with significant glances to only *certain* members of a group. Maybe you've made the mistake of hanging around with those who flatter you by telling you, for example, how thin you are, instead of those who know it doesn't matter. Maybe you've chosen friends who spread their toxic obsession with physical beauty, which is just a temporary arrangement of flesh on your face, anyway.

We discover, sometimes throughout our lives, that we shouldn't make the mistake of confusing fun with happiness, nor should we surround ourselves with those who don't know the difference. As painful as these lessons are, suffering through them doesn't even come close to the tragic pain of those who have never had a single friend.

A true affinity with another magnifies the earth's wonders to sublimity. The inside joke, the first bite of pizza, the dog snoozing by the fire, the smell of a good book, the tentative student who submits a poem that makes you cry. (You probably know who you are. I will keep that poem for my entire life.) The circle that closes around you in sorrow when you learn that, again, a full-term pregnancy is just not meant to be. The astonishing moment when you realize that your unconditional love is returned. The overwhelming desire to make yourself worthy of such a gift.

We are paying the price for replacing stories with images and thereby killing compassion. It's our individual and collective obligation to keep the fire alive and perpetuate the stories most dear to us. Let's cultivate the reading lists to keep them fresh and reserve a treasured place for the oldest, best stories that are, as we speak, threatening to sink into the deep well of oblivion. Then let's provide a sanctuary for you as students to be truly mentored—a place where you may browse and wonder, seeing what it's like to consume literature at the communal table without being devoured by the ravenous bloodcults of indifference.

Earnestly,

Ms. Gavin

What You Need to Know About "Good Country People"

Student: This story is MESSED. UP.

Friend: Dude stole her leg!

Classmate: Kinky.

Student: He was one shady snoop.

Classmate: Yet it's the perfect metaphor. It's like Jake's injury in *The Sun Also Rises.*

Friend: Yo I heard that book's about people's d%#s getting blown off!

Student: You hate to see it.

Ms. Gavin: (*Sighs affectionately.*) Whoah, whoah, whoah. We have work to do. Let's begin.

* * *

Dear Students,

I tried to warn you about the weirdness. This is a fantastic story, the perfect introduction to Flannery O'Connor.

O'Connor populates her tales with the gruesome and the grotesque, and many of her characters struggle, as she did in her own life, with deformity, disease, or disfigurement. Ultimately, O'Connor teaches us that from suffering comes that which is life-affirming. Yes, life-affirming! This Southern writer is famous for what has come to be called the eucatastrophe: a catastrophe that is necessary and good. From brokenness and the recognition of a painful reality blooms our fullness as human beings.

Think about the comedic foolishness of the small-minded people in this story. We can't look away; consider satirical memes of ardent "man in the street" interviews following break-in attempts or other disasters. O'Connor gives us the gossiping Mrs. Freeman and her voyeuristic fascination with terrible accidents. Look at the way she and Mrs. Hopewell, both aggravatingly self-satisfied, affirm each other's smug platitudes. Wince when Mrs. Hopewell's superiority complex in commending those simpletons, the "good country people." And then there's Joy.

Oh, Joy. Flannery O'Connor doesn't spare her, making sure she "lumber[s]" into the bathroom on her wooden leg. Joy has changed her name to Hulga because she thinks of herself as a highly educated, contemptuous hipster, able to truly look reality in the face unflinchingly and see it in all its terrible ugliness. Joy/Hulga would like to believe that she is completely godless and anarchic; she even goes out of her way to make others squirm and cringe by brandishing her atheism arrogantly about.

We know people like this. Cynicism is in. It has an edgy, sarcastic allure, but it too often masks the discomfort of not knowing. It's an easy way out of thinking and risking attempts at living a meaningful life.

Yet look how quickly Hulga falls for Manley Pointer, the odious and greasy huckster, with his socks slipping down into his shoes, his disconcertingly sweaty forehead, and his "Aw, shucks" routine. (And yes, there's always that one student who picks up on the joke of his name.) Joy means to seduce Pointer and shred his faith, mocking what she takes to be his ignorant simplicity. Congratulating herself for her superior intelligence and judgment, she relies, naïvely enough, on his decency. Instead of being fulfilled, however, she ends up duped, declaring her ardent love for him after receiving a few patented compliments. It is she, not he, who deserves our pity, because she has fallen under his spell, a victim of her own arrogance, ultimately realizing that he himself is as morally empty as his suitcase is of Bibles.

Pointer points Joy to reality as he unpacks his suitcase, but even more so when he exclaims, "You ain't so smart. I been believing in nothing ever since I was born!" Joy is left with her face "churning," stranded up in the loft without her prosthesis or glasses. This is the lowest point of her life. From here, she will have to climb down the loft and crawl back to the house, humiliated.

Why is she surprised? If the world, as Joy likes to proclaim pompously, means nothing and is only full of self-interest and ugliness, then Pointer's cruelty should come as no surprise to her whatsoever. Pointer easily accesses Joy's desire for love and meaning lurking just under the surface of Hulga's bravado.

Because if you really believed in nothing, you'd be just like Manley Pointer. You'd have no beliefs you felt the need to proclaim, you'd get a kick out of hurting others, and you'd incapacitate [J]oy wherever you found it, preying on the universal human desire to be loved.

Joy's eucatastrophe is a painful, necessary blessing. This is how we should see failure. Don't be so afraid of it, and don't perceive your desire to be loved as an embarrassment. Take risks in your life, and don't hide behind relativism that claims non-thinking as a form of virtuous open-mindedness: "I can't say what's right or wrong. It's different for everybody." Observe the world, take risks, and try on bold claims. Keep learning, opening yourself up to the vulnerability of possibly being wrong.

Joy can't continue the misery of her previous life as a shadow-gazer in Plato's cave. Instead of cavalierly ranting that the world is ugliness and the faithful are all just ignorant, she must become humble and accept that she is not omniscient. After all, how are we to learn anything if we are already convinced we know everything? She'll have to crawl in that door in front of her mother and Mrs. Freeman, who will dole out not just ghastly pity, but, eventually, their compassion. Things can only get better from this moment. Joy's lesson is that all her previous self-important declarations have been empty, originating from a small, loathsome, safe place within herself. Yet, in the end, her nihilism doesn't have a leg to stand on.[1]

---

[1] Apologies. I'd say that I'm better than this, but I'm really not.

With hope,

Ms. Gavin

Patriot of the Active Voice

Student: The theme can be seen in the way the literary devices are used.

Ms. Gavin: Let's consider rewording that sentence in the active voice.

Student: Okay. As shall be seen by the reader, the literary devices are used by the author. (*A classmate snickers but goes quiet when Ms. Gavin snaps him the disappointed-evil-eye.*)

Friend: What's the big deal about passive voice? I don't get it.

* * *

Dear Students,

Active voice features a clear subject, as in, "Mr. Smith closed the door," whereas in passive voice, something is the recipient of action, as in, "The door was closed [by Mr. Smith]."

One of you once protested the tenet of active voice in formal writing. Passive voice, you insisted, is just as acceptable as the active, and often preferable, especially if the writer doesn't know the subject of the predicate. You were always both a scholar and comedian, never falling into the trap of snark or superiority. I enjoyed your indignant, tongue-in-cheek message in which you declared your intent to flout the rule about active voice. What I discovered in responding to you was that this grammatical habit speaks to the core of language and meaning.

It is true that in some cases, passive voice simply cannot be helped. In the previous sentence, for example, the cadence flows better and just resounds more forcefully in the passive. Sometimes, a sentence reworded to avoid passive voice ends up reading more awkwardly.

Most times, however, passive voice can be avoided. Vagueness can be side-stepped. Accountability can be taken. Now, note the lack of active subjects in the previous set of sentences. Passive voice exonerates thoughts from subjects, that is, the *agents* of whatever it is that is causing the sentence's action.

When you write your best-selling books, pitch an idea to potential clients, or draft a contract, you will, as conscientious communicators, want credit for your purposeful language and powerful ideas. As readers, writers, and engaged citizens, we must attribute actions and words to their operators. If we don't, we might as well be Vladimir and Estragon waiting by the side of the road for our lives to happen to us.

The most egregious abuses of passive voice often lurk insidiously in literary essays, where the agent (the causer) is the author. Instead of writing, "It can be seen that symbolism is used with the father's coffee mug," train yourself to think of a literary technique as a deliberate, thoughtful, almost forceful intent of an author, as in, "The father's coffee mug symbolizes his brittle estrangement from his oldest son." Your analysis will become more astute, resounding with a crystalline certainty and purpose. In disciplining yourself to write in the active voice, you are constantly acknowledging an author's purpose. This is exactly what reading and writing help you to do in life: to listen.

Aristotle began his study of the sciences with the premise that, first, we start with the objective of knowing the first cause of things. We need our agents. He ultimately ended up with the Prime Mover. We don't have to go this far. We should, however, be able to identify a subject in most cases; our writing becomes notably elusive and vague if we cannot.

Passive voice is the language of evasion. It displaces personal accountability. And here, dear students, is where grammar shapes and speaks to our deepest psyches! Consider one of our most destructive modern fallacies: blaming others for our own missteps, assigning fault and dodging self-awareness. You failed a test? It's the teacher's fault. Missed a play on the field? Scrutinize the coach. Failing at your new job? Blame the person you replaced, and complain about the mess you inherited.

Being proactive and in control of your actions routs the pervasive notion that our self-esteem is the responsibility of someone else's whim. It's not called "others-esteem" for a reason. Know that people's high opinions of you are unlikely to fill you up for any enduring length of time. Don't become addicted to the approval of others. That's a passive way to live life indeed, to blossom under compliments and wilt under criticism. Neither is permanent, and to think so is to subject your sense of self to a violent, ever-capricious whirlwind of externals. (Just where advertisers want you.) We're all subjected to circumstances way beyond our control, but that doesn't mean your sense of self has to be so permeable. How you bounce back from troubles is a testament to your own resilience and power. That's how confidence originates from within and radiates outward. You make things happen in your own life, and you control your own actions. How terrifying. How intoxicating!

Are we not a nation of doers, not receivers? Patrick Henry didn't shout, "Give me liberty or I will just stand here," nor did Joe Wilson's famous two-word outburst on the House floor all those years ago cause such a stir because he called out, "A lie has just been said!"

If examples of zealots are too extreme, then imagine the use of passive voice in the hands of less inflammatory rhetoricians. Even passive resistance movements required dynamic organizers and proactive agents of change. To this day, passive voice is a favorite of smarmy politicians and cigarette advertisers who want to distract consumers and constituents from thinking about who is responsible.

Consider the notorious non-admission of, "Mistakes were made." Passive voice distances your readers and makes them vaguely suspicious. Let's fight against an Orwellian world where language has become a loose collection of imprecise half-thoughts that shirk meaning.

Writing not only expresses thought, but also trains and creates thought. Your world posits that it is others' opinions who shape your being. In the best cases, such a dangerous construct creates admiration addicts. In the worst, it exonerates the self from accountability in its refusal to pinpoint a decision with its subject and consequences.

Empires fall when language and meaning become divorced from each other. We need the active voice now more than ever. By participating in language, we aim to discover the root causes of human actions and meaning. Ultimately, as a writer and citizen of the world, pen in hand, you wield mighty power. It is up to you to recognize and work it.

Actively,

Ms. Gavin

More on the Non-Reading Problem: Bluff-Busting

Student: I read, but I got confused. I didn't understand it. It was confusing.

Ms. Gavin: What was confusing? What part?

Student: I can't remember exactly. Just the whole thing. (*Avoids eye contact and types on phone.*)

Embracing the Unknowing:
Socratic Seminars,
Featuring Two Fish Allusions

Dear Students,

You have probably figured out that I'm the kind of teacher who loves when the lights go out. The moment of universal perplexity. The perfunctory scream from a student in another classroom down the hall. The school-wide silence.

For one shining moment, we are one, free from the distracting hum of activity, from the whir of the air vents, from the Dementor-like, soul-sucking buzz of fluorescent lights. Every one of us wonders what happened and what this could mean.

"Yes! Embrace the chaos!" I shout, invigorated with glee. Then we go back to whatever it was we were doing before. You all always seem puzzled by my lack of alarm and the placid manner in which we proceed.

Truth-seeking doesn't require a screen, lights, or any volts at all, in fact. Since humans began clustering together, there would always be that one guy telling stories around the fire. Fear and wonder have forever pervaded our existence. Until the shadows of your life grow long, and mine has long since faded, remember this: there always was and shall be suffering, just there always was, is, and shall be, immutable love.

"We don't need some gimmick or digital device to study the true and the good!" I muse, fancying myself a rebellious James Dean, only I'm the middle-aged teacher version, smelling books in dorky straight-legged corduroys. Throw shoes in the machine's gears! We have original thought and our own power of language! Since I fancy heat and running water, I won't pretend to be a Luddite. But a noun is a noun in any language and era, with or without electricity.

One of the casualties of the twenty-first century is the spirit of shared inquiry. You've all seen it. Someone shouts, another shouts back, repeat, in 140 poorly-written characters. When I get discouraged by plunging literacy rates, the new low in discourse, and piles of grading, I remind myself that our classroom dialogues revive the ancient joy of rhetoric and philosophical questioning. Those who try to fake it by pontificating are tacitly made sheepish by the insights of your more prepared classmates.

An idea, a moment, or the wide-eyed flash of understanding truly can't be captured or created by a glowing screen. There's just no substitute for good dialectic. And great conversation can exist without a smidgeon of electricity. Socrates drove people crazy, but when it came to habits of mind, he had it right.

What makes for a great seminar? Well, dear students, you have to read, or else we skip them. Be prepared with evidence. You know to avoid upspeak (speaking? as if every sentence? ends in a question?) and vocal fry (the malaise-drenched tone of a Kardashian). Don't make conjectures about a character's traumatic past if it's not in the text. You know that if you bloviate and bestow hackneyed platitudes about, say, not judging people or being open-minded, it's going to be pretty clear you haven't put a lot of thought into the searching questions. That's a little embarrassing. You must rely on the text, truly listening to each other, ignoring the fear of being wrong. Let go of the notion that discussions are competitions. Follow the trajectory of a complicated idea wherever it may lead us, even if it's down a rabbit hole: "What do we mean by 'meaning'?"

Socrates' line of questioning befuddles Meno, who is frustrated and just wants a quick and easy answer. "You've left me feeling like a torpedo fish," Meno fumes. We know this feeling well. Two and a half millennia later, our discomfort with unknowing remains, and we tend to palliate our unease by snatching up a device for immediate answers.

Yet while technology provides distraction, it hardly offers sustenance. Don't be so afraid of being wrong or not having an easy solution. Socrates knew that the most profound questions don't have simple, pat replies, and that the lifelong quest for truth first begins with inquiry.

Socratic seminars are sacred, screen-free spaces, wherein you interact with the author, each other, and the world's greatest questions. It takes a while to get it right. Practice distinguishing between what you think from what you feel. It's no easy task. Initially you might all turn into cage-match beasts, competing for points, so you might give answers you think a teacher would want to hear. You may be hindered by your own discomfort about not knowing everything. Feeling torpedoed, you may rush to fill the space with words, terrified of the silence.

And how I love awkward silences. I feed off that psychological discomfort and devour it ravenously like a rabid parasite. (Does anyone remember the 70s horror film *Piranha*? At one point the piranha, in their high-pitched frenzy, actually EAT THE RAFT of the screaming camp counselors.) The longer the awkward silence, the better. Feed me, Seymour! Relish a thoughtful pause, I urge you. Here is where the mind races, the external noise ceases, and the author speaks.

Lights out? Bring it on. Water main break? We'll make it work. Power grid out on the eastern seaboard? We got this. Let's slow the fevered pace of our interactions. Give snaps where snaps are due. Nod thoughtfully for each other. Embrace the chaos, I tell you. Don't take a text's difficulty as its unknowability. Welcome the discomfort of grasping for noble ideas just beyond our reach.

Yours,

Ms. Gavin

Green Centuries,
Ray Bradbury,
and the Necessity of Myth

Dear Students,

    I love distributing new books to you all. Although a lot of you may not be into reading, I enjoy the way the air vibrates with the promise of undiscovered ideas. Questions, called out and unspoken, saturate the room, even if it's just to wonder, "In what ways will this book make my life miserable?" Many of you complain, but in some of you, I can sense an undercurrent of curiosity: is this the book that will speak to me? Finally? What's it about? What's with the picture on the cover?

    Some of you go right to the end to get a page count. Others inspect your copy for defects and fish through the remainders for a better one without bent pages (even though I promise they all end the same way). While I stave off your questions about whether or not there will be a test on the book and try to activate your imaginations with enticing stories, I notice that a few kindred spirits sniff it. And we know there's nothing like the pulpy smell of a book.

When I first began discussing *Fahrenheit 451* with you many years ago, you were thrilled with Ray Bradbury's vision of a futuristic America. No books? Mega-sized interactive television screens in each living room wall? Twenty-four hour headphones? Score!

Some were excited about the novel for the wrong reasons, but your responses typified the phenomenon about which Bradbury is writing: the compulsive addiction to what he calls "factoids," represented by the constant blinking digital image with no primal source, journey, or emotive destination. Screens act as a narcotic, mesmerizing us with flashing pictures and sound bytes that come from nothing, signify nothing, and are lost in eternity once they vanish.

It was at a summer course about epics at the Dallas Institute of Humanities and Culture (and I promise this is going somewhere) that I first heard about *Green Centuries* by Caroline Gordon. The scholars who had read this novel about the settling of the frontier during the Revolution raved about it. For years, however, my copy of it remained on the bookshelf unread. Whenever I skulked past it, I averted my eyes guiltily, the way one does with haunted orphan books one buys but never reads.

At some point, however, it reappeared in my thoughts and I felt it calling out to me from the collective unconscious, telling me to read it because now it was time for this story.

What I discovered was that *Green Centuries*, framed by an incredible introduction by Thomas H. Landess, is the American epic nobody is reading.

Rion Outlaw's search for freedom on a new frontier is also an abandonment of any established human community requiring him to answer to other people. Throwing off what he sees as the shackles of an ordered *polis*, Rion chooses a quest that both permits and requires him to turn his back on social order. Maybe many of you relate to his unquenchable thirst for the everlasting elsewhere. His call to move west has a might of its own; his heroic-demonic urge isn't satisfied when he arrives, for there is no such thing as wholeness. Rion is most fulfilled on the way there. He prefigures Theroux's Allie Fox in *The Mosquito Coast*. Clearing the land with his bare hands for hours on end, Rion becomes wholly absorbed in the visceral joy of altering the environment and building himself a settlement. He is ever driven, as Gordon's last lines suggest, to find an oasis and destroy all that makes it good.

Cassy, the mother of his children, senses Rion's drive to keep moving further into the frontier, but treasures what they have built together. She craves roots and stability, and Rion is her ruin. Love has drawn her to Rion, but is not enough to ground him and keep his wanderlust in check, particularly when he hears Daniel Boone's stories. (Many of us may at some point find ourselves in her position, drawn to someone whose loving gaze will never be fixed in one place. Cassy doesn't get out, but you still can.) Whether it's the pursuit of power, adventure, or anything else temporary, Gordon reminds us that conquests take their toll.

As the novel's heavy current draws its characters to a tragic conclusion, interpolated chapters tell the story of Rion's brother Archy, who has been assimilated into the Cherokee nation. In her admiring portrayal of the Cherokee community, Gordon presents a culture with highly sacred bonds of human kinship, full of significant images connecting the people to each other and to their ancestral past. Archy's contentedness is from being "there," a symbolic and literal location of "nowness" where every human action signifies a complex system of rich, totemic meaning.

By the end of the novel, we feel the gravity of history's pull toward the future and away from a shared and cherished past. The arrival of preachers who aim to establish a church does little to assuage Rion's restless yearning for the wilderness. As Cassy prepares for a celebration of what will be the settlement's first prayer services, she gathers berries for pies and, with a full heart, makes plans to feed the those she loves. In retrospect we realize that this will be her last scrap of happiness on this earth.

Cassy pays the price for Rion's call; she is Dido, doomed to love fiercely and lose catastrophically. *Green Centuries* is at once about an inspired beckoning toward something greater and the consequence of losing oneself in the quest, resulting in the decimation of the best virtues that sustain a civilization.

This is the American epic. We need stories about the necessity of community and the importance of social tradition. In the same way that Ray Bradbury's Mildred is filled with desperate hysteria in front of the chattering screens but feels no real connection with her surroundings or kin, we are all on a frantic hunt for something better. Mildred is missing what Rion is seeking but ultimately destroys: reconnection, in a postlapsarian world, with each other, with the land, and with the Creator.

Many of you equate modern, centerless suburban developments with something you vaguely sense is missing, but what is actually missing in your lives is not just a front porch or Main Street. It is story. Myths connect us to who we are. Social media platforms are poor substitutes for the assiduously prepared meals Cassy serves her family, or Old Lanthorn's gift to her husband—a tapestry depicting the entire community's values. The lives of these women will be changed by the unappeasable, Cimmerian restlessness of others, but for the moment they find peace in the absorption of continual, time-consuming acts of giving.

Readers of *Fahrenheit 451* may be able to connect the book's themes with the creepy isolation of being able to use ATMs, customer service, and drive-throughs for weeks on end without ever having any human contact. We can get a speeding ticket, order groceries, straighten out our cable bill, and donate furniture without communicating with a single other person. And why would anyone want to create a phenomenon whose joys they haven't experienced? I've asked you all what draws you together with other people, and what stories have shaped your worldview. Sometimes you answer that watching a popular reality show unites you, but this shared experience tells you nothing about who you are as a person, much less to what heights you should aspire yourselves. We need better stories by which to live.

What I am going to say next runs counter to current mainstream thinking: we must be careful about revising our myths and eliminating them because of unpalatable facts. These are dangerous waters. Demeter's loss and Washington's cutting down of the cherry tree may be apocryphal, but they tell us about who we are. Cultural myths do not have to be true to be real. If we tear down a story, we must replace it with something. Even stories of our unpleasant past are dark mirrors that reflect our collective identity and speak of where we come from. They are too important to cast aside.

So this is why I love passing out new books to you all. While many of you are cynical and closed off to reading, you are secretly hungry for books to mean something to you. When you anxiously check your phones over and over, you may be searching for something real you can't even name. When you receive a new book in English class, being curious about what happens (as if story were about plot!) is only on the surface; on some level you are curious to find out who you are, what the world is like, and how you fit into your larger cultural fabric. Many people aren't aware of or nudge aside these yearnings, even though humans have felt them in dreams and in uncanny waking moments ever since we crept out of the primordial ooze and started making marks on dark cavern walls.

Books like Caroline Gordon's *Green Centuries*, with its understructure of classicism and more overt theme of human connections, beseech us to read them. We have to give the next generation the gift of myths and heroes, for future archaeologists will assess our civilization, not by the luxuries we were able to amass and how quickly we were able to move, but by the values relayed through our shared stories.

Myths save us from the abyss of self-absorption, exciting a grand marvel that calls to each of us. How we answer the call leads us to our destinies. If we ignore it, our tepid or tortured destinies find *us*, and we are listless by the time they arrive. We need to revive our culture with the elixir of good stories about what it means to be human here and now.

Fervently,

Ms. Gavin

Poetry Teacher Cleans out the Lost and Found

Bloated corner box lopsided and seething with abandoned
items:
Trees in the breeze, tropes and trochees,
A scrap of living life to the fullest,
"Life" rhyming with "strife," and, by the way,
Does he know she exists?
Patched spondaic britches,
R-rated epithets for edginess
(cynicism has always been in).
Now she is elbow deep:
alliterative bluebirds and gale gusts.
Dig a little further, find a striped symbol in fleece,
pull out a wrinkled simile as old as the hills.

She cannot throw them away.

They can epistrophically linger longer,

mingle, repeat their endings,
grow nostalgic over their earnest beginnings.
She refolds the items with care,
tucks the box away,
and writes a poem.

Reading the World

Soul-Depleting Narcissism and April's Epic Wound

Dear Students,

We've all met people who ask how you're doing only so they may tell you about themselves. I wonder why grown people at times seem to think you pass them in the hallways not because you are heading somewhere, but because you want to hear their catalogue of woes. In these cases, "How are you," becomes a dangerous question, because one is then likely to hear all about why that person thinks his or her life stinks.

I don't mean healthy venting or complaining. I mean the circuitous ranting that feeds on itself and doesn't go anywhere productive. If you say you are busy with work and have to go—in a rush, can't really talk right now—they attempt to give lengthy anecdotal evidence that they are actually the busiest individuals in the building.

Depending on the environment, some workplace hallways are a minefield, and you've got to dodge the emotional vampires if you can. Don't get sucked into their vortex. Whenever you try to put up psychic shields by rushing past them and explaining that you're swamped with no time to chat, they might change direction and declare, "I'll walk with you," so they can traipse along, muttering about their lousy lot in life. You'll have to be strong, dear students.

When did we stop listening to each other? I'm sure Adam and Eve conversed in the Garden, drinking in the sense of connection that comes from truly loving somebody. They didn't take turns ranting and using each other as emotional sponges. It could be that they didn't even have language, because they wouldn't need words to bridge a rupture that had yet to exist. Maybe they even spoke with one voice, until that forked-tongued serpent got in the way. Then once they got kicked out of Eden their relationship jumped the shark. Now they had things to complain about and stopped really listening.

A common lament after people go on first dates is, "He only talked about himself. He didn't ask anything about me." We've all been in those conversations, maybe with somebody whose sentences start with "I" and end with "me." How draining, to be around people whose presence requires the heavy lifting of keeping the conversation going when they don't possess the tiniest inkling of curiosity about who you are. What's troubling here isn't just that people aren't taught to show concern for one another, it's that they so often don't *have* concern for one another. It doesn't occur to some people to wonder about anybody else. Instead of, let me see whether I get along with this stranger, or, is he a potential friend, they ask themselves, how does it feel when I project onto this person? Whenever narcissists gaze at you intently, it's only to search your face for their own reflection. Don't ever put up with being anybody's mirror.

Have you ever been in or overheard conversations like these?

— I was in the emergency room with severe head pains. They say it might be a tumor.

— Yeah, my shoulder won't stop bothering me.

— My son is desperately struggling with major depression; we've tried everything. We just can't go on like this. (*Eyes well up with tears.*)

— Welcome to the club. My husband is still addicted to *Game of Thrones*.

— Please help! I've just dropped an anvil on my foot and I'm badly injured.

— I get blisters on my big toe.

I'm cranky.

T.S. Eliot wrote that April was the cruelest month. Dear students, you are often mystified about how this could be.

It's not just allergies or, for you, the flurry of college acceptances and rejections (don't get me started on why this frantic system is injurious to you, your families, and our society). April is a time of rebirth, but think about the epic wounds of buds forcing their way through limbs that have been sleeping in murky, dark somnambulance for months and months. It's a beautiful violence, harsh and meek. Life is a willful force; it edges itself and its verdancy into a world that, although brutal, necessitates rejuvenation. New life cannot exist in a closed environment, nor can thought, for both will feed back on themselves incestuously, wolfing down any real sense of truth, sustenance, or beauty.

I'm hoping that my peevish annoyance will be replaced by something more nourishing, something that spreads a warm glow of joy to those who are in danger of wallowing in the chasms. Please remind yourselves that the earth is ever turning toward or away from the sun. Right this very moment, good things are happening that no human could possibly see. They are happening deep within forgotten crevices and lonely abysses that have been covered with sad snow and ice all winter.

I've said it and I will always, always mean it: love never goes away.

Sincerely,

Ms. Gavin

What Will I Do with My Life? Hopefully, Many Things Having Nothing to Do with Each Other

In my mid-twenties, I worked for a children's book publisher. As a lifelong reader with unrealistic ideals about the workplace, I was bound to become disillusioned. Our resources were dedicated more to merchandising for an unpublished manuscript than to the books themselves. Aspiring writers: if your children's manuscript isn't compatible with the potential of a stuffed animal, tv series, and fast-food tie-in, I may have bad news for you.

Don't think I'm on any kind of moral high ground, though, or that I was unhappy there for ethical reasons. There's not a thing wrong with selling or marketing. My co-workers were geniuses, experts in human nature who knew how to create dreams and deliver them. Mostly, I didn't like working in an office, period. Deep down, I'd always wanted to teach.

My apartment was only eleven miles away from my job in midtown. That's an astonishing feat for one's first apartment in New York City. It would have been more miraculous had my daily commute on the subway not been an hour and forty minutes each way.

I tried to make the best of subway time, getting to know the performers on the N line. Those urban troubadours were true artists. I wish I could tell you stories about what my favorites sang, but those songs are theirs. Mostly I willed my brain to stop trying to identify random stenches. I read Faulkner and listened to my Walkman, trying to find the subway glamorous. Sometimes I got a little maudlin listening to the "Field of Dreams" soundtrack and thinking about poor Addie Bundren's fishy, decaying body.

After a year, they raised my salary to $26,000. Now I could splurge for the bus on special occasions for a dollar more each day. It was more civilized, especially if you got the good driver who loved his job and sang out each stop with lilting panache: X27, I'm in heaven! Colonial Road, get off the commode! Third Ave, the ex took all I have!

My sister will tell you that I still get a residual adrenalin rush when I see the X27 pull up to a bus-stop in the city. My heart starts palpitating, and, if it's the express, my fists clench and I prepare to run, ready to elbow my fellow humans aside. Every cell in my body becomes eager to knock people over like wheat stalks falling before the churning thresher, just to catch that bus and get a good seat. The express doesn't play around.

Along with my raise, they gave me my own office. I was honored to be its first inhabitant, as it had recently been a facilities closet. No one ever notified the custodial staff of the change, so the supplies just kept coming. People wandered in looking for Windex, bleach, or the vacuum cleaner. Sometimes they even knocked.

Most often they came to reach just around the door and take a roll from careening towers of toilet paper. It was a great way to meet people, and I tried to help the visitors as best I could when they wandered in. I didn't mind when someone came for the plunger, just when he tried to return it. Really, it wasn't the worst set-up; all those boxes of restroom supplies provided sound-proofing. It was as if I had my very own padded lair, perfect for hibernation.

Windows were over-rated anyway. At the time, I was living in a Brooklyn studio with one narrow window that looked out onto a dank alley. Someone on the fire escape had shot a BB gun into the apartment twice. Thankfully, the BBs didn't reach their destination; they only made two holes through the exterior pane and were stopped by the interior one. Every time I opened my window, the two pellets rolled around, knocking into each other and clicking in the narrow ridge between the two panes of glass. They were doomed to roll around and look out onto the sooty-bricked alley, trapped forever. I knew just how they felt.

At the publishing house, I tried my best, but I wasn't a very good assistant to the editor. Ordering and cleaning up her lunch was easy, but I made callow mistakes like placing her mail in her desk's in-box. As a worker, I was always on time and stayed late, but surely there must have been times when my threadbare perkiness just wasn't enough to conceal my misery. The reality is that I was too inexperienced and immature to come up with inventive ways to make my boss's life easier every day. Looking back now, I see that I was probably, actually, pretty terrible.

It wasn't all bad. We got to take part in the New York Book Festival. Our company marched in the parade and featured several booths, so we rookies pulled from a hat and dressed up as popular characters from children's' books. Much to the disappointment of my friend Ethan, I drew Dorothy from *The Wizard of Oz*. I dug it at first: wig, make-up, checkered dress, basket with fake Toto glued to it.

I walked alongside a television chef's float in the parade, blindly flinging stale candy out into the audience. My aim is terrible, so I hope that all ended up well. Once I ran out of toffee, I raced from booth to booth moving books, distributing promo kits, and breaking down boxes. When the festival ended, we still had to disassemble the stands and transport everything (risers, books, tables, standing marquees) back to the headquarters in midtown. By the time I got back to the office late that night, my floor was locked up and the lights were off. I'd have to wear the costume home.

The ensemble must have cost a fortune, so who knows what hit the company took there. Because by the time I got back to my apartment, there were entire chunks of sequins missing from my ruby slippers. I looked like Dorothy took a walk on the wild side before trying to claw her way out of a panic room. My wig had lost a braid, and my grungy dress looked like a tablecloth at a hoe-down for the criminally insane. Toto had been decapitated. It was the day the New York City subway outclassed me, and no one on the commute home even blinked.

My building's super liked to sew, and she tried to help me fix the damage as we sat in her cozy basement kitchen for our nightly chats, watching over her sleeping grandson. At one a.m., I looked forlornly at the pile of tangled thread and sequins on my lap. I was making it worse. Toto's severed head had now lost an eye.

I put down the glue gun and pitifully confessed to Sonia what I had never said out loud.

"I hate my job."

"Ees okay, Mami," she said, patting me on the knee. "I hate mine too."

On the bright side, at work I became the liaison between the author and illustrator of a children's book about potty time and toilets. Just what a lifetime of great literature had prepared me for. Move over, Tolstoy.

In a job you hate, one that fills you with dread and turns your stomach in knots, there will always be that one day. The breaking point. Some call it rock bottom; Joseph Campbell would call it the belly of the whale. I will tell you about mine. It was a Tuesday.

My sales calls, mock-ups, and photocopying were backed up hopelessly. I had to assemble and ship out marketing kits, two-hundred seventeen, to be exact. About the same number of dollars that were drifting around and bumping into each other in my cavernous bank account. I also had to continue the unsuccessful saga of trying to get to the bottom of suspicious charges on my boss's credit card from her vacation. Plus, I was expecting a massive paper towel delivery any minute. You get the idea.

On that day's dash down to the art department, I'd try to figure out how to tell them that, on page seven of the proof, the urine in the toilet was just a little too dark for the author's liking. It needed to be less yellow. I'd have to be tactful with them, and more so with the artist, who was already perpetually indignant about her artistic integrity and refusing to come out of her studio in NoHo.

I lost two hours in the morning because of a meeting in the boardroom where the topic was whether or not pee-pee and poo-poo should be hyphenated. How did Strunk and White not foresee this dilemma of our times?

That afternoon I got lost in Central Park on my lunch break. I found myself at the site of the very carousel where Holden Caulfield stops running away from everything, moved to tears by the sight of his little sister. So I mean it when I say that there I found myself. Good old Phoebe. Going around and around on the merry go-round, sunnily waving every time she passes her big brother. Holden can't catch her and preserve her innocence. He can barely catch himself. And I knew with certainty that I too would lose myself and drown. Unless I became a teacher.

Anagnorisis, you guys.

That story has a happy ending, so far. If I ever master teaching, I'll let you know, but I understand it's not possible. Every day on the drive home, I kick myself for the missed opportunities and the things I should have done better. I fuss over how I can possibly squeeze in more without sacrificing depth, or wish I had finished that stack of papers. There are days when I get so frustrated I age a decade, and there are days when you students crackle with insights, thoughtfulness, and exuberance.

I've said before that, as your teacher, I'm neither friend nor therapist, but this doesn't negate my concern for you. I wonder why you don't do your homework, why you don't eat breakfast, and what I can do to get you to nod in quiet understanding during a class discussion. I'm troubled when I hear more from your parents about your grades and missing assignments than I do from you, or when I realize that I'm working way harder than you are. I send good vibes to the student who worries too much and has yet to realize that, come on, most people never feel as if their true selves show on the surface, anyway.

Most days I think about the student I can't reach, and not necessarily the one who tries the hardest to display as much loathing as possible. (No you can't keep your head down and no you can't go to the bathroom.) But you in the back row, shoulders hunched as if you're preparing yourself for the next onslaught of life's barrages. Over there, the one trying not to cry publicly from lack of sleep; why do you spend so much time on minor assignments, always pressuring yourself to be perfect? You care so very much. You're staying up until 2 a.m. to work on one paragraph, aren't you? Grow your confidence from the inside out and believe in your inherent value; I want you to have a joy and sense of self that doesn't need the stamp of an A+. And you on the side row, who hasn't ever liked a book—yet!—your very demeanor suggesting that your existence is something for which you must apologize. I see you.

I gave up my silly notions of what happiness looked like. It's a lot quieter than I thought it would be. And so much better. All of you, read and write your way there so you can love what you read, figure out who you are, and articulate just what you mean. No one has everything figured out, and you should stay away from those who claim they do.

Know that things work out, whether we worry about them or not. When I come home, my husband knows what kind of a day I've had the second I walk in the door. And then my dog Lolly tackles me, and I know that everything is going to be okay. It will be for you, too.

Tartufo Man

Dear Students,

In the midst of my befuddled first year of teaching, my friend Stella brought opportunities to my door and pushed me to take them. We taught at the same school in Maryland almost twenty years ago now. A musician and a mystic, Stella teaches everyone around her whether she means to or not. Stella could be at a café in Alaska and run into her sixth-grade lab partner or kindergarten teacher. It is no coincidence, because she is that kind of person. She is in sync with the universe.

Here is the first uncanny scenario I will recount for you. About fifteen years ago, Stella and I attended an academic conference on Beauty at Notre Dame. We were on campus hoping to meet up with Stella's brother Patrick. It was the pre-cellphone era, but we still hadn't thought far enough ahead to find out where he lived or how to contact him once we got there. Knowing that Pat was a student at the School of Architecture, we headed to that building. The place was enormous, and it was packed. Classes were letting out and the hallways were crammed with students.

We headed to a stairwell, where Stella tugged the sleeve of one passing student and asked, "Do you know Pat?"

"Yes, he's my roommate."

The second uncanny scenario with Stella was later on during the same trip. A gaggle of us needed to get to a conference dinner but had no ride. We were lost, straggling along on a deserted street, when out of nowhere a crowded bat-mobile zoomed up. It was a clown car full of the Catholic intelligentsia! The window rolled down and a scholarly head emerged.

"You must be Stella!"

"And you are S——, who wrote the book on architecture that changed my brother Pat's life!"

"We're headed to the dinner. Hop in!"

There's a third coincidence I will tell you about, and this one is my own.

Pete's Tavern is a family tradition. Whenever my father, sister, and I are anywhere near Gramercy Park, we head to Pete's. For years we got the same waiter. He was stubbly, surly, and disdainful, and we ate it up. We became strangely attached to this harried man who clearly loathed us. Rolling his eyes at our stupid menu questions and throwing the check at us as if he were hawking a loogie, he was our favorite.

The three of us conducted long conversations speculating about his life story. His accent sounded vaguely Eastern European, and he would always stare at something just beyond your shoulder. We wondered if it were the past. My family and I hypothesized about what was bothering him so much, and whether or not he would be our waiter again in the future. Fingers crossed!

On the few occasions when he wasn't our waiter, we felt disappointed and betrayed, insulted when some other waiter smiled solicitously and took his time explaining the specials. The nerve of that guy, asking us how we were enjoying our meal.

This is how our favorite waiter came to be called Tartufo Man.

One night at Pete's Tavern, my father had a craving for some ice cream. We asked for a dessert list, awed by the incredulous sneer this brought from our waiter. My father is a man of cultured sensibilities but an old-school taste for uncomplicated cuisine, and he grumbles when menu items aren't in English. If we're eating at an Italian restaurant, for example, and the menu items aren't in English, he mutters, "Spaghetti this, spaghetti that!" So when our waiter began rattling off the night's desserts, rendered unintelligible by both his accent and the fanciness of the items, my father interrupted him every time he heard something that sounded anything like "ice cream."

Dad: Do you have ice cream?
Waiter: (*Exasperated sigh.*) Tartufo, tiramisu, eis ——

Dad:	(*Hopeful.*) Ice cream? Ice cream!
Waiter:	(*Labored heave of shoulders. Why must I*
	deal with these cretins?) Tar*tufo*, tiramisu,
	Irish cream—
Dad:	Ice cream! I'll have that.
Waiter:	No! Tar**TUF**o...

It went on like that for some time. After that we never saw our guy again at Pete's. Maybe we pushed him to his breaking point by making him say "tartufo" eleven times (I counted). We often ruminated on his long-suffering soul, thwarted aspirations, and torturous dealings with the Gavin family. He entered and left our lives with a stomp and a flourish.

Several years later the three of us went to the Metropolitan Opera for *Tales of Hoffman*. Our visits to the city without seeing our favorite waiter had become a little wistful. As we pulled into the parking garage of Lincoln Center, we found ourselves handing our keys over to the parking attendant— Tartufo Man! I believe I exclaimed that when I spotted him. His face lit up, and we all chatted about how he used to work at Pete's Tavern. He was really quite nice.

Since then my family and I have concocted elaborate theories about Tartufo Man's move. Moreover, we have talked about what a small universe it is for such a big city. If something like that happens, the world is in its rightful alignment, just for one suspended moment.

Coincidences have always suggested to me that the wheels of the cosmos are turning, and that all is right with the world.

Things are clicking into place. We can't see what's behind that veil, but sometimes we intuit whispers of its workings. The turn signal blinking in precise time with the song on the radio probably means nothing. Maybe on a granite island eleven miles long, running into your favorite populist hero isn't unusual. Statistically, however, it would be extraordinary indeed if all these things signified nothingness. Even our intrigue about the possibilities is miraculous all by itself.

The more you read, the more catholic human truths you'll encounter, all expressed in astonishing variety. You'll start to find common threads among, say, Aristotle, Rumi, and the current drama going on in your friend group. You'll connect Jane Austen's world to the highly-mannered realm of promposals, and be amazed later on when see what Faulkner does to that feminine ideal with Caddy Quentin in *The Sound and the Fury*. We marvel when the universe snaps into order for one satisfying instant.

Are these connections all haphazard moments that exist in an isolated, context-less vacuum? Well, why do we so often vehemently insist that they must? We shouldn't deny ourselves suppositions. After all, it's possible that everything we know in this world is an advanced alien life form's sixth grade science project. He probably got a B-; his work with gravity, foliage, and free will were ingenious, but he lost points on our lack of harnessing renewable energy and on the problem of evil. I mean, it *could* be…and doesn't it delight us to imagine?

Wondering about possibilities is one of our greatest gifts. One of my favorites is more likely than the alien science project: that we're all connected, and that our experiences are woven into a cohesive tapestry of storied ideas far too complex for any one person to fathom. Together we ruminate on the cosmos and its options.

Whenever people discuss faith of any kind, we inevitably hear the old condescending refrain, "People just need something to believe in…" Then the retort, "You just need to believe that people just need something to believe in," and so on. Yet something's inscrutability shouldn't be evidence of its non-existence.

If we declare that only what is known exists, we aren't just killing dialogue. We are also making gods out of our logic and limiting the entire universe's possibilities to that which our minds are capable of calculating. Our puny, gooey little brains, which wouldn't be working out at the intellectual gymnasium because we'd have ceased wondering and trying on theories. And wouldn't that be a boring, arrogant way to live one's life, without rumination, mystery, or the great conversations pondering what it's all about? It's such fun to suppose.

In chaotic times darkened by a growing, vacuous pessimism, strange glimpses of order remind us to gaze upon the possibility of infinite marvel. We don't have to meet this magnificent entirety face to face right now. If we did, we probably still wouldn't believe. Maybe we'd even be prone to scientifically dissecting and destroying it to comfort ourselves with a false sense of ownership and superiority.

Dismissals of coincidences fall in line with the cynicism that we postmoderns enjoy brandishing. Yet look what happened when my family and I honored Tartufo Man by hypothesizing fondly about his life. Our desire to name and identify with a stranger speaks to the necessity of human interconnectedness and meaning.

We don't always need to see it. Sometimes, just knowing it is there is enough.

Not Coincidentally,

Ms. Gavin

Missing

It started by glancing at clocks with feverish exasperation,
wishing away weekdays and waiting for lunch,
or Fridays,
or spring.
Mondays were sloggish, the unlived days hard on their
shoulders.
They called Wednesday hump day.
They hated that Sunday night feeling, so they amputated it.
But then Saturday bled through.
They lost the calendar.
Friday night snuck out the back door to grab a beer
and never came back.
Sunday morning self-imploded when, having no ceremony
upon which to stand, it
wobbled feebly and collapsed, resolving itself into a Thursday.
The days melted through their fingers, slid down their bod-
ies,

and pooled at their feet in congealed puddles
of primordial Tuesday goo.
Brittle November was dumped on a hat rack,
but shattered when it toppled over;
it was up to December to sweep up the shards.
February packed up, lugging his shabby valise of winter
and taking the decade with him.

This is how things end,
By chunking up seasons and years so they may be discarded,
along with you and the other good things I wished away so
often.
They disappeared,
just as readers race toward the end of the poem
and nudge it into the past.
It recedes into a digitized vanishing point
before blinking off,
before becoming gone.

Working Itself Out:
Three Good Conversations
and a Terrifying Plane Ride

2012. A first date. Dinner at a restaurant that used to be Haven in Pleasantville, New York.

Ms. Gavin: So you're a pilot. (*Looking for reassurance from a pro.*) I tend to be a nervous flyer…what's the deal with turbulence? Is it really that dangerous?

Bruce: Oh yeah. That'll kill you. Snap your neck right in half. Wear your seatbelt at all times.

Ms. Gavin: … (*Marries Bruce three years later.*)

* * *

Dear Students,

So the other day in the hall, I got into a discussion with several of you about fashion. Sometimes you enjoy my anthropological curiosity about your lives, and you cheerfully inform me about the latest trends. I'll never understand how to use your slang the right way, but I do so enjoy the dorkiness of getting it terribly wrong every time.

Anyway, I was asking a few young ladies how you got your jeans to tuck into boots without having the 80's mushrooming out over the top like Mindy's denim did in a "Mork & Mindy." You didn't understand that, nor did you get it when I likened the look to Crissy Snow's of *Three's Company* fame. But one of you did a helpful demonstration.

"It won't all bunch up, though?" I asked.

Your answer resonated with me, long after I realized you didn't have a hall pass.

"No," you said. "It just works itself out."

I don't have a fear of flying, just of crashing. "Safest way to travel," people declare with a nonchalant shrug. In college, two VMI cadets assured me that even if every engine went out on a plane, a good pilot could still land safely. I tried to remember this advice a few years ago on my way home from Dallas as I boarded a flight to New York one rainy, windy night. Only, I saw the pilot on my way in. He looked more like the Fonz than Sully.

The older gentleman next to me in 25C asked me about the book I was pretending to read, G.K. Chesterton's *Orthodoxy*. I say pretending to read because I was actually fixated on the captain's announcements, scrutinizing them for signs of danger. His statement about buckling our seatbelts for heavy bumps ahead sounded overly brusque and panicked to me. I studied the movements of the flight attendants, interpreting their bored expressions as highly-trained poker faces, façades masking their deep and mounting terror.

Mr. 25C wanted to know what my book was about, and showed me what he was reading, the *Tao Te Ching* by Lao Tzu. It turns out he was a retired teacher and school administrator. We talked about our books, marveling at how they both addressed the same questions—what is our purpose on this earth? How do we live a just, peaceful life? As 25C and I compared, the uniformed naval reserves private next to us got in on it. When the turbulence became heavier, I turned to him for reassurance.

"You're in the military, so you must go through this all the time," I said.

"Not really!" he exclaimed in a panic, tightening his seatbelt and clutching his tray table. His wide, rolling eyes resembled those of a horse trapped in a burning barn.

My seat-mate in 25C seemed to understand things. He asked me if I were married. At the time, no. Got anything lined up? No? Well. "Don't ever think you're the only one out there. It'll happen."

These conversations would normally default to the script of how it's hard to meet the right man, just living life optimistically, and so on. I know a lot of women who would need no further prompting to ramp up into a "Guys These Days" tirade. Students, please avoid from getting caught in this looping narrative. In this situation and in life, resist the allure. You know the one: the cliché of heady outrage. Although we've all come across people who have behaved dishonorably, it's disrespectful and soul-damaging, to yourselves and to others, to assume that all members of any particular walk of life can be denigrated and dismissed.

Miles above Pittsburgh in a metal tube wobbling and hurtling through the air, my mind ran through a previous set of disappointments. I mentally drifted through things about my life I wanted to change, including the fact that, at the time, I didn't feel like a New Yorker and dreamed of a warmer, slower place below the Mason-Dixon line. I thought about my life's goal—to be ever surrounded by good, smart, fun, compassionate people—and realized how abstract that actually is.

Mr. 25C was still waiting for an answer to his question. I made a flippant comment about dating, something equivalent to the offhand, "Safest way to travel."

My new friend paused before admonishing, "No hiding." He must have sensed more than my tendency to hibernate in the winter. The plane descended in jerky increments, and I winced when we dropped. Everyone knows that gripping the armrests actually helps to keep the plane in the air, especially when it's accompanied by a sharp intake of breath. My seatmate turned to me with advice that would have made Lao Tzu beam with serenity.

"Just go with it," he said.

At the end of *Troilus and Criseyde*, Geoffrey Chaucer releases his book into the world and hopes that his beloved creation will live a long and fruitful life of being understood without misinterpretation. There is a sad, stabbing beauty as he declares poignantly, "Go, little book." Chaucer is proud of his offering, but he must also relinquish command of it. He's telling it to work its works, acting with faith because no author can ever really control critical reception or reader interpretation. Having lovingly created something beautiful, Chaucer must now let it go.

Sometimes we can think and think ourselves into a corner, when we, too, just need to let go. Reading Chesterton with a pencil in my hand was not going to tame the wind outside the plane, nor was making a dissertation out of the flight attendants' facial expressions.

We may scour volumes of theology and attend university lectures on physics, geometry, Debussy, Aquinas, or Van Gogh, voraciously seeking and gobbling down information in efforts to understand this world and our place in it. We pilgrims tend to pace the earth to and fro, restlessly searching, cramming days with mileage like frantic nomads. (Do we cultivate gratitude with this much tending?)

During times of sorrow, some seek intellectual comfort as a way to comprehend grief or think away suffering, as if understanding pain in all its scientific faculties—causes, symptoms, solutions—would abate it. Sometimes, however, we just need to throw ourselves off the mental hamster wheel and wait, even if that means letting go and resting in a liminal place for a while. We can hope that our meaningful words and actions, sent out into a cosmos that is beyond our comprehension, will bring about good things.

Go with it, dear students.

Things just work themselves out.
Go, little book.

Significantly,

Ms. Gavin

Audrey Hepburn and Living Marble

It's true what they say about the light in Rome, and I cringe a little to tell you that, many years ago, I was the girl writing in her journal at a café when I first visited. I roamed the city for hours on end ("without a Baedeker," as Forster would say), and found a plastic Saint Joseph statue that I got for my dad, who was trying to sell his house. Saint Joseph is the patron saint of real estate, and, according to legend, a home seller is to bury this statue upside down the back yard to bring about a speedy sale. This seems to me to be an undignified way to treat a religious icon, yet ostensibly it expedites the house-selling process. Antonio from the "I Love the Vatican" gift shop, you've got yourself a deal.

Audrey Hepburn, as Princess Anya in *Roman Holiday*, serenely and boldly declares to the press, after a significant pause, that Rome was the favorite part of her European tour, making meaningful eye contact with Gregory Peck's Joe Bradley—the dreamy, roguish American newspaperman with whom she has enjoyed her Roman escapades. It's a

Grecian urn of a relationship. If I were a princess with an entourage, and had stolen away for a taste of freedom from regal duties to romp around town and cause a little good-natured havoc with the locals, then had to leave dreamy, roguish Gregory Peck because of royal responsibilities, I definitely would have told the press, upon returning, that my favorite part about my travels was the *Pietà*.

Eager to avoid crowds, I got to St. Peter's early in the morning, and I found myself in the quiet basilica alone. I stood in trance-like wonder before the marble sculpture, and something stole over me that has never left. I don't know whether anyone reading this has ever seen it, but the sculpture quite palpably glows.

Rough and hard marble, chiseled from a massive quarry chunk, and smoothed to a luminescent sheen, has been rendered translucent. The Madonna gazes down at her son's limp and heavy body, contemplating the once-was, and her face is full of unfathomable love, sadness, and inscrutability. She looks so young, maybe because love and loss this profound transcends time. This is what no mother should have to endure.

Michelangelo was a man of love. He may not have wanted to paint the Sistine Chapel, but he spent years on his back making it beautiful. In St. Peter's, this flesh that cannot be marble, but is, glows with the *gravitas* of the human condition. We are all doomed to leave this earth, and to lose those dear to us. For those who may be uncomfortable analyzing the *Pietà* in religious terms, the masterpiece still evokes the human reality that we will love, lose, and be lost during our time on this earth.

What a burden it is to endure such sorrow; multitudes of men have been driven mad by the thought of impending mortality. Marilynne Robinson's John Ames faces his death by writing achingly luminous, tender letters to his young son. Achilles rages and sulks in his tent, resisting his fate of death, holding up a war for years and thereby ensuring his legacy in the realm of storytelling and myth. Death finds him, but so does the immortality of story. What a gift this is.

In the procession of time, youth is just old age in its becoming. We outlive the songs of our parents. But we can still sing them and create melodies worth passing along to future dreamers.

We create, we lose, we laugh and suffer. We breathe in our stories, myths, music, art, poetry, and each other. We experience moments of being taken out of ourselves when we see something that echoes the great beauty. Our time is so short, yet our laps are open to nurture, comfort, and mourn those dearest to us.

Standing in the presence of greatness makes us wonder about our own legacies and what to do with our fleeting, temporal moment (inhale, exhale) in this pageant of eternity. As for me, I'd be content if I could ever make anybody consider the grand, illuminated procession of which they are a part: the larger story of their cultures, legacies, and dreams. Too often we see each other in instrumental terms, as opposed to Kant's ideal of seeing each human being in light of his or her intrinsic value.

The ways in which we react to beauty may say something about each one of us. How dispiriting that some lost soul was once wretched enough to take a mallet to the *Pietà* and damage the very face of the sublime. Were the statue to be destroyed, would it cease to exist? No. At the very least, it would leave behind a relief in the air it once occupied.

I've often asked my students what would happen if every single copy of a book were destroyed (and they have fun imagining which books they'd happily subject to such a fate). Those stories, I posit, still exist on a celestial plane of our collective unconscious. Those words are just waiting to be called back down and re-assembled from the psychological, spiritual stratosphere into which they have atomized.

For Audrey, it's Rome. For Harry Potter, it's his Petronus, and for Samwise Gamgee, it's Frodo. We all have our familiars, our beloveds that speak to us. They anchor us to our deepest selves and inspire us by beckoning us to truths we have yet to discover. My familiar is books, realms in which it is I who am liminal. Books and the *Pietà*. What is yours?

Critics and cynics alike may take their own stances on the *Pietà*, maybe because it's situated in St. Peter's, as far away as possible from hip secularism. Maybe they scoff since they think idealized depictions of motherhood are obsolete icons that subjugate women, or because they consider the sculpture an over-rated, touristy bit of tripe. Yet if you ever get the chance to see the *Pietà*, postpone any political ideas it might support or deny. Let yourself be taken out of time. Gazing on the *Pietà*, I see something so full I don't even have words for it. It gets me every time. Whatever it is, I sense that this is what it means to be human.

Ubi Sunt?
Or,
Where Have All the Cowboys Gone?

Dear Students,

"Back in the day" has entered your linguistic currency, and speaks to our tendency to long for the distant past, one deemed much preferable to the present. We are ever feeling like we just missed out on an era of purpose and greatness. In Guido del Duca's tirade against Tuscany in Dante's fourteenth canto of *Purgatorio*, we find a catalogue of the old heroes. Starting at line 97, he "weep[s]" when he thinks about the good men of the old days. Similarly, Marco of Lombardo in canto sixteen reflects on three senior citizens "in whom the former age reproaches the new" (lines 121-2). These guys are the last living legacies of the older, better ways.

Do you remember *Little House on the Prairie*? Recall Almanzo in mustard-colored, high-waisted corduroys that are too tight, orange plaid wallpaper in Oleson's General Store, and Ma Ingalls' chic hippie dresses. The show's take on the frontier says more about the seventies than it does about the era it depicts.

In the same way, even with its claims of authenticity based on extensive research, *Mad Men* may tell us more about our modern era of pitching, buying, and falling than the nineteen-sixties. Cacciaguida's reminiscence is 1320's version of a bygone era of good men and modest women. It was a simpler time.

Even though many criticized Reagan's leadership when he was in office, his biographies now fill bookstore shelves, coinciding with Reagan allusions in political speeches from both sides of the aisle. Woody Allen's film *Midnight in Paris* reflects our affinity for nostalgia; a writer venerates the Lost Generation as a time of the greatest writing and innovation, whereas the members of the Lost Generation look back to the Belle Époque as the Greatest Era Just Lost.

Maybe every generation sees itself as just having missed out on something great, except for the self-nominated Renaissance era, where they certainly knew and took pride in their mammoth contributions. The nostalgic tones of Cacciaguida, del Duca, and Lombardo seem to resonate through the ages to our own times, wherein we bemoan, not just the distant past, but the recent past with fondness and a yearning melancholy.

Books like Tom Brokaw's *The Greatest Generation* venerate the veterans and civilians of the forties and fifties for their heroism and character, with each chapter devoted to a different individual and their struggles and virtues. Released the same year, movies like *Saving Private Ryan* and the miniseries *Band of Brothers* also call on the merits of the previous generation.

Of course we idealize the past. Like a book whose entire story sits enclosed between its two covers, the past is set safely in its untouchable timeline with outcomes we internalize as historical facts. My father, for example, reminisces fondly about his childhood, shaped by his Irish neighborhood in northern Manhattan during the forties and fifties. As little girls, my sister and I loved listening to his stories, wishing life were as simple as playing hide-and-seek in Inwood Hill Park. Whenever we expressed longing for that better time, Dad warned us against romanticizing the past. "It was also a time of fear," he said. "As kids, we had drills where we had to hide under our desks in case the Soviets dropped the atomic bomb on us. Can you imagine having to do that type of thing now?" Well, about that…

My father witnessed people waking up during the Civil Rights Era, but also the inconsolable moans he heard when attended Dr. Martin Luther King's funeral. Dad describes his community's terror about polio and visits to the local dentist, a.k.a., "The Butcher." No time, he reminds us, is ever trouble-free.

We are fortunate if we recall our own childhoods with affection, as I do about growing up during the seventies and eighties, which are now enjoying a pop cultural revival. Teenagers may feel as if they've missed out by not growing up in the eighties, and of course I agree. In our household, we had one television set in our basement on a rolling tv tray. The two handles for VHF and UHF were missing, so we turned the channel with a pair of plyers. If the reception were too snowy, we rigged up the rabbit-ear antennas with tin foil. Even better, if you were a younger sibling, you got the privilege of being the signal conductor, because you'd stand holding the antenna waving one contorted arm in the air until the reception suited your sibling's favor, at which point, you'd stand frozen like that until the show's closing credits.

For a solid year, we pestered our beleaguered father, unsuccessfully campaigning for an Atari game system. He had no choice when Grandpa gave us one for Christmas anyway. It came with one game: Pong. This is where you watched a square dot bounce from one side of the screen to the other. We were astonished by this modern marvel, transfixed by the trajectory of the white dot moving back and forth, back and forth. Hours of wholesome fun. Two weeks later, the spell broken, we went back outside and never touched Atari again.

Technology wasn't interesting enough to keep us inside all day. The eighties felt like morning in America, and we talked about it with each other on avocado phones in our floral-papered kitchens. It was a time of Prince, *The Goonies*, and the smell of fresh crayons. But it was also a time where we feared Gaddafi, acid rain, the Russians, and a strange, frightening disease that people were calling "gay cancer." The good old days are couched in the past, but because of our view of our own place in time, we like to linger on the best aspects of it, even as it slips away moment by moment.

Maybe the phenomenon is as simple as human beings not appreciating the present, just as a child might have the tendency to complain about going to camp all summer long but misses it the instant she returns home. We become attached to the near yesterday that is becoming ever distant.

Your parents may feel this obsolescence acutely when they allude to, say, *The Love Boat* or *Reality Bites* and get no flash of comprehension from the younger crowd. My dad felt it when he first realized I didn't know who Erroll Flynn was. Our reaction to your blank look isn't exasperation, but a wistful realization of time's passage.

Your children may not know who Kanye is. Maybe they'll listen to your stories about the good old days of SnapChat, libraries, and Netflix, before the complications of digital brain chips, unforeseen global tensions, and the extinction of bees. We don't have to live in the past and dread the future, just keep the present moment in our minds.

In Dante's *Purgatory*, Marco of Lombardo, a soul doing penance, stops to reminisce with Dante about yesteryear, particularly the heroes he remembers from his youth. Marco gets annoyed when Dante doesn't know about great men like the venerable Gherardo, but then Cato calls him back from the naughtiness of idly chatting by what amounts to the office water cooler. Marco is schooled about time in a constructive way, reminding all of us that we shouldn't let our earthly ambitions get in the way of our atemporal ones. We are all small glints in the well of time.

Dante's souls in Purgatory cannot squander time in dawdling and gossiping when they should be using it for self-improvement, and neither can we. Nor should we waste our time vegetating before screens, which won't provide memories you'll yearn for nostalgically in your old age.

In the distant future, will you wax poetic about the Instagram account where you saw a model posing with her elbow on her hip, jutted out just so to make her arm appear thin? Or the innumerable photos of others in the exact same stance? Are you going to miss that, or any other of the inane images of someone you don't know as she, say, brushes her teeth wearing lipstick and a tiara?

The twenty-first century obviates significant interactions with other human beings. Technology doesn't always bring us together or make us more mindful. It often becomes the vehicle through which we engage in self-absorbed identity-crafting and sidestep meaningful exchanges.

Social media taints poignant life experiences with the intrusive impulse to take pictures and offer them up for public consumption. Don't seek approval or envy from people you barely know or from those whose good opinion actually means nothing. Lose yourself in timeless moments, becoming fully immersed in their utter sense of completion. If you interrupt them, make sure it's only to send some of that good energy to your future self, because there are times when you'll desperately need warm memories. Don't put joy on hold just to update your status: "Marge is making macaroni and cheese! Trout pout and peace symbol!" Throughout your life, create moments that are worth missing, and don't kill them by stopping to record them or show them off online.

Marco learns that his stay on the terrace of the wrathful is better spent working off his own sins instead of what amounts to cosmically insignificant chit-chat. We could do with that reminder, too. Here in *Purgatorio*, where the spirits need no snarling watchdogs between each permeable level,

Marco of Lombardo disciplines his own interactions with the world. He is learning the right way to think about time and his own place in it. Dante's episode instills in Marco the truth of time's preciousness, just as all of *Purgatorio* reminds us that here on earth, we exist in the realm of time.

Our affection for the recent past places our longings at our Tantalean fingertips, combining our memories with our hopes. We don't reside in Augustine's City of God, where the instant and the eternal are identical, coexisting as one. Reading, like reminiscing, is comforting because we see the narrative in its ordered, self-contained finitude.

Nostalgia is our way of linking ourselves to the procession of time, of grounding us in the before-, during-, and after-ness of our own lives. Indulging in the bittersweet banquets of memory may help us synthesize the distant past, the recent past, and the enigmatic future. Those places provide imaginative diversions, but we just mustn't dwell in any of them for too long. We need to be our own taskmasters to remind ourselves that we each exist in the present, within the bounds of the momentary.

Remember the nineties, with their combat boots, plaid flannels, and Pearl Jam, when everything smelled like teen spirit? Before we had CNN, GPS, or Tinder? Remember last Thursday at dress rehearsal? Or the curiosity of seven minutes ago when you were just starting to read this chapter? Or Eden, when we needed no gatekeepers at all and didn't know sin?

Living the march of time, we wonder what is to come. What could possibly be next? We try to picture futuristic cars, cleaner air, taller buildings, and odd silver clothing. It's healthy to imagine the future, just as it is to cherish the past, but both need to stay in their rightful places. Make your life worthy of the next generation's nostalgia; give them a world that will inspire them. Right now we are living the goodest, oldest days of them all that will provide us, in dark times, with regenerative, glimmering warmth and light.

Sincerely,

Ms. Gavin

Hysteria One, Discourse Zero

Dear Students,

Years ago I took you to the auditorium so you could watch the inauguration on the large screen, excited that you'd witness such a milestone in history. When the former President appeared, several boos and jeers erupted from the crowd. A few stray pieces of garbage flew up at the screen. Some students listened to the speeches; most played on their phones.

Back in the classroom, many of you were justifiably proud that your country could arrive at this new breakthrough. I wonder, however, whether we are prematurely smug about our open-mindedness and inflated sense of being more highly evolved than other generations. Before we congratulate ourselves on our job well done, maybe we should consider the ways in which we brew up and unleash toxic and irrational vitriol.

We fail to respect our leaders or each other, but then get affronted if we feel that we're not the well-respected or popular kids in the global village. It's always easier to criticize and destroy, but are we setting good examples for the next generation about how to conduct a thoughtful, productive discussion? Is anybody listening? Or are we carried away by the intoxication of cynicism and throwaway comments about how someone or something sucks? The delight of spirited conversation, the aim of which is personal connection and insight, has been replaced by the narcotic rapture of disdain.

Private venting among friends has given away to public tirades. Being brash about one's opinion seems to have become more important than the opinion itself, shoving aside the search for the truth and the ability to speak reasonably. The new administration had built a platform on diversity and tolerance, but it's hard to reach across an aisle that's snowy with spitballs coming from both sides.

We have talked before about how apathy and its close cousin, illogical histrionics, are destructive to a democracy. Both indicate that citizens aren't asking questions, watching their leaders, or making decisions in a careful, thoughtful manner. Many of you are probably thinking about the recent elections, but I can guarantee you, the next one will be no better.

It's hard to believe that Lincoln and Douglas debated for hours on end. Voters didn't have commercial breaks or screens; they stood listening to the whole thing, following complex arguments on both sides. Sometimes the candidates would break so the spectators could have a meal, then reconvene and resume their debates. Imagine everyone's masterful attention spans and avid curiosity.

Both hatred and delirium for the President are merchandisers' dreams. They count on consumers riding the riptide of strong emotions with their screens on and their wallets open. Hysteria makes for a better economy, since idealists and rage-aholics both relish sharing their feelings with bumper stickers, t-shirts, and coffee mugs, whereas the apathetic just don't care.

Know that there's no substitute for being educated and taking the time to digest the facts. Irrational behavior is a great money-maker, and I'm sure the Trump-bashing bumper sticker factories are the same ones cranking out the Clinton-hating banners, presidential bauble-heads, and commemorative spoon sets. Don't buy any of it. Just listen.

Best wishes,

Ms. Gavin

Not with a Bang,
but with a Whimper

Natural disasters? Locusts? War? Mere fleas. It's red tape that will ruin us. I've seen the future, and here's what it looks like when you try to communicate with those who don't speak the language of story.

Gavin:	Hello, hospital finance department. This is my ninth time calling over this June bill that was already resolved with insurance. Two months ago, after several calls and letters, you and I came to that conclusion together. Can you please check your notes?
Hospital admin:	No notes.
Gavin:	Yes, please check your notes.

Hosp: That's not what I have here. (*Forty minutes later.*) Oh, now I see the notes. We have spoken on numerous occasions. Who am I speaking with? No, it says here you owe us.

Gavin: Yes, you'll see I spoke with you, Marcia, and Jan, but now, despite agreeing that I am not responsible for the bill, you have submitted it to collections.

Hosp: Okay, ma'am. What is your profession?

Gavin: I'm an English teacher.

Hosp: (*First and only signs of enthusiasm throughout entire conversation.*) I *HATED* English!

Gavin: Okay.

Hosp: I don't really read.

Gavin: Not even when you were little? There was no book you liked? How about Dr. Seuss's *The Sneetches*? I loved that book.

Hosp: (*Awkward pause.*) Our records say you owe us. Would you like to put that on a credit card right now?

Gavin:	How about *The Great Gatsby*? You probably read that in high school. Those were some parties!
Hosp:	Oh yeah, that's the book about the boats. It had Leonardo DiCaprio in it. Will that be MasterCard or VISA?
Gavin:	I feel like the pair of green pants with nobody inside them. (*Crickets.*) Can you please read your notes? (*Silence.*)
Hosp:	It says here, "Decision to charge patient was overturned."
Gavin:	Right...and "overturned" means—
Hosp:	We'll have to look into this. We'll call you back, but it might not be this week. (*Click. Sends another threatening letter.*)

To think that Gilgamesh and Aragorn did great things without having to fill out a single form.

Seven

The beginning of her is a pulsating globule, a speck of light.
Pressing her tiny face against the crib slats, she yearns and
hypothesizes about beyond.
Later, in pigtails, she dreams of swing sets, fireflies, moon-
beams, and starlight.
Seven wonders in pictures, dreams of candy, tries to fly in
meadows
when she has a good running start.
She is lit from the inside out.
Wants to be a nun, a singer, a writer, plays with words and
thinks in vast, vague, dictionless images.
Ponytails now, and porcelain dreams.
Her heart still leaps when she hears
the ice cream truck.

After seven, the eggshell of her
waxes paper-thin, then becomes concave.
Now she retreats into her room and thinks in numbers,

ones about herself that are
never small enough.
She is peering out,
not from crib slats,
but from the wispy bonecage
of her angular tiny-ness.
She ignores the residual
heart leap
when she hears the ice cream bell outside,
imagining only
to speculate about
how she is seen,
pinching her stomach,
little Seven's little entirety no longer
a straining bud
but a crepe shell
as she trudges along the bottom of the ocean
and the atmosphere presses on her
from all sides.

Super-Teachers and
Euclid's Reluctant Hero

Has anyone else ever cried over math problems? Raise your hand if you have done so in the past week. Nobody? Oh. Um…me neither…

There's something about not understanding math that feels so urgent. Essays feel personal, but math is linear and marches ever forward, nearly zombie-esque in its steady, undeterred trajectory. The curriculum just keeps getting more advanced and you feel stuck as everyone else whooshes way past you. It's like being awake at 2:37am when you feel like the only human on the whole dormant planet who isn't sleeping soundly.

In seventh grade, I was the new kid in a small New England town where very few people ever moved in or out. Weeping over math was nothing new; I had done so in Maryland, too. When we moved to Massachusetts, I was way behind. What was long division? I didn't fully know the times tables, and still have to think hard to remember them.

It was Mrs. Paull (math teacher, ballroom-dancer, world-traveler, cookie-connoisseur) who saved me from crashing. This super-teacher stayed after school with me every day to work on problems with clarity, patience, and warmth. Mrs. Paull knew that I needed a lot of math remediation. She also knew and cared that I had no mom to go home to after school.

There was one shining moment when other students were jumping out of their seats in eagerness, calling out wild guesses to answer a question no one could get. When I mumbled meekly, "Null set?" from across the noisy room, Mrs. Paull activated her supersonic hearing and cried out, "Who said that? THAT'S what makes a mathematician!" I went home feeling as if the entire school had paraded me around their shoulders in the town square, chanting my name.

As a teacher, I think about my own teachers every day; classroom moments remind me of their mannerisms, how they handled things, and the interesting stories they told. Who wouldn't be inspired by the glamorous Mme. Beaton, who took us around Paris with an élan I could never hope to describe or possess? I often think about how I wouldn't have survived middle school had it not been for Mrs. Paull and the very dear Ms. Capone, two teachers who helped me so profoundly that I can't really write about them for some reason. When I moved up to high school, I knew I would miss my super-teachers, but in a way I still felt their cocoon around me.

I coasted through the first day at Canton High School without being particularly taxed. We learned about rules, played get-to-know-you games, and talked about our summers, while secretly wondering who would be in our classes all year and conscious of our first-day outfits (big hair, Champion sweatshirt, and, if you were lucky, black Guess jeans pinned at the ankle). Easy day. Then came period 5. Algebra.

Ms. Leshefsky was all business. She handed out our math textbooks curtly, and, in a clipped tone, directed us to open our notebooks. My friend Drew sitting next to me put his hand to his temple in slow motion and mouthed an expletive as he slunk down in his seat with dread. It was going to be that kind of year.

Ms. Leshefsky was one of the best teachers I ever had. Boy, was she terrifying; she was both stern and sprightly at the same time. We loved her.

She was always moving. We never saw Ms. Leshefsky seated; we hypothesized that she graded our tests while running on the track while making breakfast while contemplating the mysteries of the galaxy. Nobody was ever late for her class, ever. My CHS classmates of '92 may appreciate the magnitude of my racing from history in A-building to algebra in C-building *with time to spare*.

When Ms. L. got a new haircut in November, I ventured a compliment. I meant to say, "Your hair looks good. It's always nice to have a change," but what came out was, "Your hair looks nice for a change." Oh, the humanity.

There was the day I was working on an article for the newspaper during algebra. What on earth was I thinking?! Nobody did that with Ms. Leshefsky. She was solving an equation at the board with her back to us, but stopped and sniffed the air suddenly, her elfin head cocked to the side. There was a disturbance in the force. She knew.

Ms. Leshefsky took the paper from my desk and walked it to the back window, opening it up as she scanned the paper's contents. She wasn't angry, nor was she ever, because she was always in control. Ms. Leshefsky never had to yell; on this occasion, she was tightly, mildly interested in what it was I'd dare to work on. Resigned, I told her to throw it out the window, and not because I was being defiant or calling her bluff. I just suddenly realized that my piece really was terrible. Getting busted gave me a fresher, more accurate view of reality. Ms. Leshefsky just kept talking about solving for x and patted my paper down on my desk pointedly on her way back to the board.

By December, I loved algebra. Solving equations was therapeutic, and I just wanted more. You have to understand how revolutionary this was. Math still never came easy to me, nor does it now. I have a strong sense of direction, but if you were to tell me that a street is four-hundred feet away, I have no idea what that means. Eleven yards? 8 kilometers? Interchangeable to me. I can tell an inch from a foot, and that's about it.

If you tell me to turn left about five yards down, then go straight for thirty feet, I'll be polite about it. I'll even squint and nod in appreciation for your time. But internally I'm just eager to move on, already entering the address in my GPS. So when I tell you that I looked forward to doing Ms. Leshefsky's homework in high school, your jaw should fall open in shock. Mine certainly did when I saw the A on my report card.

We all desperately wanted to do well for Ms. Leshefsky. It was extraordinary how deftly she could manage the energy of the classroom; there was no down time, but Ms. L. kept us on high alert without making us anxious.

Winking beneath Ms. L's stern demeanor was a subtle, impish humor. No question could ever throw her off, and for the rare student's attempt at meandering off topic or goofing around, she had a swift, lively retort. Her smile was quick and genuine. What a triumph when, the day after she attended a Rolling Stones concert, we got her to put on her Mick Jagger t-shirt! It was the talk of the cafeteria for weeks.

When I published an article in the school newspaper about dropping my older sister off at college, Ms. Leshefsky went out of her way to tell me how much she liked reading it. She said it brought a tear to her eye, which, she emphasized, never happened because she didn't possess human emotions. I knew better.

Some kids are lucky to have one teacher like this; I was blessed to have several and I wish they knew how much they did for my life. At the end of the year, Ms. L. asked about my writing again, and complimented my participation in the school play, where I headlined as Chorus Girl #12 and Lady with Shopping Cart. Talk to my agent. Even though I was in the back row onstage and quiet in class, she made me feel seen. Thank you, Ms. Leshefsky.

My dys-math-ia resurfaced at the Graduate Institute at St. John's College in Annapolis. We read Euclid, writing out his proofs and getting philosophical about geometric space. We did Lobachevsky and Hjelmslev, working with infinity.

Chester Burke, genius professor and flautist, can tell you about my math meltdown when I learned I'd do the proofs for everyone at the board the next day. He sat cross-legged on the table before me, encouraging me to let it out and marveling with enthusiasm at how math anxiety speaks to our very depths. I got through it.

Mr. Burke once asked me to write about the *story* of geometry. Story? I perked up. Breakthrough! Mr. Burke must've seen me sneaking sniffs of Euclid's *Elements* during class. It's awesome when a teacher just *gets* you.

Poetry is to prose as geometry is to algebra, calling for a different way of "seeing." Personally, to truly understand the emotional truths of just about anything, I need a story.

So let's choose a shape to ponder, maybe the one that most closely resembles a delicious slice of pizza. Given Euclid's love for order, is it possible to see his proofs about this figure as poetic? At the very least, they are philosophical, a vision of the cosmos as Euclid perceived it. Another way to put the question is, what is the story of a triangle? It's imperative for me to answer this question and make Ms. Leshefsky proud of me.

The first book of Euclid's *Elements* commences with definitions, opening credits introducing the *dramatis personae*. From this list of main players, one might assume that it is the line, or even the circle, who will be the story's protagonist. In fact, the first proposition suggests that Book One will feature the circle, with its Mother Earth capacity to produce an infinite number of equal lines emanating from its center, perfect and justified in its symmetric roundness.

After all, constructing an equilateral triangle with radii from the circle's center seems to speak more to the fertile capabilities of the circle than to the incidental potentials of the triangle. Book One, however, follows the journey of the triangle, a figure introduced a full four definitions right after the smug circle. In Euclid's first book, it is the triangle's mystique that illuminates the world for us. Like math itself, the triangle simultaneously shuts us out and touches on the boundless.

Let's consider the triangle as one line, cracked twice until its extremes touch. It's the first straight-edged, closed shape we can create. Since it's the first enclosed area we can construct with straight lines, the triangle would appear to be the simplest figure. Yet a triangle embodies an inscrutable inviolateness; in all of its varieties and possible measurements, it still possesses the same number of degrees as one straight line. Its brokenness just makes it stronger, more fortified against, as the Prince of Denmark would say, the rays and segments of outrageous fortune.

Furthermore, it is all angles, and when we try to get inside to understand it (as we have with a circle and its radii), we get elbowed out, relegated to understanding it by gazing upon it as outsiders. We can determine whether or not triangles are equal (a task whose importance is revealed later on in the story), but even to understand its interior, we must first be content to be mere marginalia. Geometry makes us abandon the first person: it's not all about us. Learning, after all, requires us to suspend our egos and identities as we gaze up at giants.

Initially, Euclid examines the sides that bound a triangle so he can calculate the equalities of its guarded interior angles. Even then we are merely determining how two triangles relate to one another; there's no activity within the triangle itself unless we're bisecting it, in which case we're only creating another enclosed triangle that we still can't enter. Oh, you want to split me in two? Try it, and I'll come back at you as three. I'm waiting.

Proposition sixteen proves that an exterior angle is greater than either of its interior and opposite angles, and proposition thirty-nine allows us to extend two sides of a triangle to make the angles under the base equal to one another. By producing these lines further away from the figure itself, we can divine qualities about the triangle, but we're still regarding it from the outside. When we get to climactic proposition thirty-two, the great revelation of the story, Euclid demonstrates that an exterior angle of a triangle is actually equal to its two interior and opposite angles.

The triangle, in its innumerable variety of forms, regardless of measurements, exhibits a universal, eternal value. The Euclidian triangle frees us from our traditional notions of shape, offering us a sense of hard-won permeability. Its wariness has forced us to produce an exterior line, and here, then, is our way in. Here is where Math and English are soul sisters. How beautiful—its difficulty makes us *create*. When we create so that we can understand something, the subject starts, like a journal entry, to work with us.

We have to practice math and writing inventively, tenaciously approaching it from all angles. Such tasks squelch any funny ideas of passivity. How very like life itself: understanding something difficult won't ever just wash over you. You'll have to engage it. Stuck on a tough reading passage? Feeling stagnant in your job? Not getting along with somebody? Try approaching it from a different angle.

While geometry resides outside of space, Euclid establishes a sense of location. His words provide not only a channel between the interior and exterior, but also a demarcation of space invented by his language, grounding the triangle to a region. Proposition five claims that isosceles triangles have equal angles at the base. In the midst of this floating, hypothetical space, Euclid gives the triangle a place to sit, and a place for all of us to rest our gaze. Who says chivalry is dead?

We tend to imagine that a triangle, unlike a circle (which floats free from direction) can be upright. The *reductio* in proposition seven is based upon triangles "on the same side of" a line, as if a line cuts space into two zones, giving us a sense of orientation. Euclid, then, portrays the triangle as dignified by a particular *gravitas* that doesn't weigh it down the way it does, say, the point or the line.

Euclid only reveals how this enigmatic, three-sided figure may be a portal to the perpetual after leaving the arc of the triangle's story to explore parallelograms. These figures are comprised of lines that, like Keats' lovers on the urn, are destined never to meet, ever. If we trust postulate five, parallel lines touch the infinite, residing in the realm of never. Parallel lines that do meet at some point, as proposition thirty-nine claims, are in fact not parallel and are imperfectly spaced.

Still, it must be a lovely reunion, two lines slanted so slightly that it takes eons of microscopic leaning for them to find each other. It's nice to ponder, unless you're a Lobachevskian, classifying lines as cutting or non-cutting. Such an encounter guarantees a showdown. Those two lines are going to have a swordfight, and *someone's* getting cut.

So while a triangle itself is closed and calculable, it stands on its base as a threshold to something sublime. Euclid's previous propositions suddenly come into crystalline focus as we see his masterful planning: two equal triangles situated in a particular configuration will create a parallelogram. The fixed traits of sides and angles making triangles equal have the potential to create shapes bounded by lines that, when we are compelled to draw them, will never meet.

Here, then, is the heroic appeal of the triangle in Euclid's first book. Like the teachers who shaped me and were my base over the years, the triangle is tenacious and fierce. Just as my teachers who gave far more than the job required, the triangle's finitude still points to infinity from within its closed self.

The *Elements'* protagonist cannot be a circle, a square, a line or even a point. Existing initially in the conceptual realm of Forms, the triangle may at first appear lopsided, off-putting, or obtuse. Yet, like many things we try to understand, it is devised of universals and speaks to something asomatous, gingerly yielding a brief glimpse of the eternal.

Ms. Leshefsky, wherever you are, thank you for pushing me and seeing me. Thank you to all the teachers who knew that their calling transcended a paycheck, went way beyond an eight-hour work day, and dipped into eternity.

Gimme shelter, Euclid. Paint it black and wait on that friend. Rock on.

Down with the Research Paper

Dear Students,

The research paper though. The research paper! I may lose some of you with what I say next, which is that the literary research paper is a tedious dinosaur it's time to either rework or retire.

There is a time for all things. There was a time for saddle shoes, and there was a time for Victrolas. As Kevin Bacon reminds us in his impassioned *Footloose* speech to the city council, there is even a time to dance. There was a time when students needed to learn how to use the card catalog, ditto machines, Encyclopædia Britannica, and the microfiche. (Parents, do you remember staring at that dimly lit, humming box, using the knobs to scroll through blotchy articles?) There was a time for the literary research paper, and now its time has passed.

No one should stand in the way of content that teachers love and have kept fresh and relevant for you. For teachers who love the research paper, please rock out to the great Stevie Wonder on your next commute to work: Teachers, keep on teachin'! In many cases, however, we have stuck with the research paper because it has become a habit or because the curriculum requires us to. We keep dredging it up and inflicting it upon you in six long weeks of note cards, outlines, drafts, and articles about what other people say the book means.

There's inherent value in letting you choose a topic you like and conduct research to learn more. What's better than being in charge of your own learning? I'm protesting the brand of literary research paper that asks students to read a book, then dissect literary criticism to get to the heart of its meaning. Many of us are already over-reliant on the opinions of others. More of you routinely look online to see what a book signifies instead of reading it closely and thinking about it yourselves.

Now, it can be helpful to read what others scholars write, so you can see how it's done. Some articles will be beautifully written and insightful. If you love reading, you'll enjoy reading literary criticism and, yes, do it for fun. In the secondary classroom, we just shouldn't start there when it comes to interpreting a book.

Googling is automatic. What doesn't come as easily is searching for the work's deeper truths independently, and coming to your own conclusions about what an author is trying to say. That's the challenge we're avoiding when we turn to a screen.

The premise that you students don't know how to find information is laughable. For many of you, the actual book is the last place you go, if you ever get there at all. When you skirt around a book by reading tidbits of online information here and there and grasping at fragments of class discussions, you're not yet ready for a literary research paper. You'd get nothing out of it. First we need to help you develop your concentration and become a stronger, more mindful reader.

You've probably heard other teachers lamenting the loss of focused, prolonged reading and writing. Students writing a literary research paper in the 1970s didn't suffer the distraction of cellphones and computers. Go back further; until the twentieth century, writers penned their books longhand. Their readers devoured books in long, uninterrupted chunks of time. Can you imagine?

When you can understand and interpret dense texts confidently, you're more equipped to arrive at abstract philosophical conclusions about them. You get better and faster with repeated practice, but a lot of you don't get or go for that opportunity; we've talked about all the distractions that fracture your attention spans. Such sophisticated skills will take a long time to develop, and they'll require a dramatic recommitment to help you get there. Ideally, this reinvigorated dedication starts with you, but it also needs to be encouraged by your family, your friends, your teachers, your community, and the global village. We should all be encountering books and writers *everywhere*.

After students of yesteryear reached the milestone of reading and re-reading the book itself, they'd then head to the library's wooden card cabinet with a pencil and slip of paper, looking in its tiny, squeaking drawers for available CLC volumes and photographed articles from academic journals. Do any readers remember getting lost in the stacks?

We're in a different era now, and it's a terrible mistake to perpetuate the tic of instantly looking elsewhere for answers instead of thinking for ourselves. In the English classroom, our primary focus as educators should be helping you read carefully and interact with authors. Engaging in all sorts of practice, both guided and independent, you should devour a wide variety of core texts, without the sieve of online commentary, and ruminate on their own words to discover their secrets. Understand that literary criticism is someone's educated opinion, but not one on which you need base yours. Imagine having the confidence to formulate your own insights before seeking shortcuts.

No, no, some may insist, students need practice synthesizing outside information with their own ideas. True. Yet you must come to the table with your own ideas to begin with. To research literary criticism when you haven't yet had enough practice reading and assessing a book on your own? You first need to read that book carefully, perhaps more than once, and arrive at your own conclusions about it.

Teachers and families should furnish you with plenty of time and space to wonder, discuss your impressions, freewrite, and ask profound questions about a text. Otherwise, the literary research paper doesn't close the gap between synthesis and original thought. Why? Because you are so habituated to bouncing around various websites looking for the right answer that you haven't gotten a chance to develop your own voice.

You certainly know where to look if you're seeking, say, "inspiration" for a paper, or an insightful observation to offer in class about a book we're reading. Some students may even have the misconception that consulting online analyses is a virtue, thinking it shows initiative and wanting to make sure they're "on the right track." I say this without judgment, and out of genuine concern, dear students: some have been doing it for so long that they think they're actually working.

Yet while going online for answers demonstrates frenetic action, it only sidesteps the harder exertion of contemplation. We've substituted deliberation and diligence for skimming and spraying our gaze around everywhere except the text itself. We're so afraid of ourselves.

Given the chance to think quietly, we rush to fill the silence with *doing*. Type, search, point, click, skim, repeat. What we end up with is an indistinct potpourri of para-phrased plagiarism. Maybe you change the online words around just enough to make them sound original. More in-nocently, maybe you've gone to several sources, so you've come to think of the amalgamated analysis as your own. Thus your perspective about the book has become inextrica-ble from what others have said. In fact, blending a variety of online ideas has become so second nature that the word "plagiarism" may even have startled you just now.

You simply must be given breathing room and quiet time to improve your literacy and take advantage of every mo-ment. Educators must help you with what you need now, not what we needed back when we were teenagers ourselves. Otherwise, we might as well teach you how to operate a tele-phone switchboard, edit documents in MS-DOS, and excel at LBJ's Presidential Fitness Test.

St. John's College, with campuses in Annapolis and Santa Fe, is a forerunner of the Great Books movement, wherein students read original texts—Aristotle, Plato, Darwin, Hobbes, Achebe, Marx, Austen, Lobachevsky, Lincoln, Hegel, George Eliot, Euripides, Wollstonecraft, Jefferson. You won't encounter modern voices here except for your preceptorials, but you'll read so much that you'll begin to visualize a trajectory of influential thought emanating from ages past. A strong foundation in what came before changes the very way you read, no matter how modern a text may be.

Delving into the ideas of core texts and Socratic discourse, without consulting the analyses of "experts," Johnnies trust that a work's own author is the most reliable source of meaning. How novel! Engaging directly with a writer almost makes too much sense. If you enjoy seminars and want to engage with prodigious thinkers without the noise of trendy interpretations, then I urge you to check out this remarkable school.

In public education's fixation on research and looking anywhere but within for answers, we have made you students too dependent on what someone else says the work means. We've talked before about the dangers of becoming an approval addict. In college and in the world beyond, you'll have to read closely and think deliberately, independently, about the text right in front of you.

We seem to have relegated author intent to an afterthought. I doubt you'd want your own life's works to suffer the same fate. And, no offense, I've seen your outside sources. Hamlet's struggle with his primordial nature?

Please. That idea wasn't even that unique (or on target) when I first read it twelve years ago.

Many people have tried to change my mind. Someday it might happen. But so far, nothing has been able to refute what I see in the classroom every day. Students today need more time and practice reading original texts deeply. Not just for information, as the Common Core would have it, but for meaning, profound thought, and depth of knowledge. For compassion, cultural literacy, critical thinking, innovation, inspiration, and for the sake of humanity. It's our direst imperative.

Yours Truly,

Ms. Gavin

Why Dante?

Just a quick word before you read on: why Dante? Some of you have asked why I constantly write about this giant, and why I have Dante-inspired artwork all over the classroom. What does the sign over my doorway mean ("Abandon hope, all ye who enter here")? How come I bring up Dante every day in class and in life? When Professor Lindia comes in to talk to you about Dante with his fiery, inspirational virtuoso, why do you think we end up yelling and practically tearing our hair out with fervor? Read Dante and you'll see. He's everything.

I tend to go through phases where I become fascinated with something and immerse myself in it completely: sculpting, slingshots, knitting, guitar, painting, quilting, soccer, motorcycles, drawing, and various historical eras. I do the same with authors. My attention is intense and not always long-lived, but I always come back to Dante.

The hypertextual anecdotes in each line of Dante's poetry say everything about his world, suffering, and omnipo-

tent justice. From catastrophic personal losses to ruinous political turmoil, Dante lost everything that ever meant anything to him, yet he wrote his way to redemption. He had
every excuse to lapse into self-pitying nihilism, but he turned
his suffering into art.

Despite such devastating grief, Dante could actually con-
ceive of and represent a world that still made sense. Close
readers recognize something universal about the painfully
imperfect pilgrim who became a Poet when he re-aligned his
soul with the scope and depth of the Creator's love, which
has crafted him (just as he is!) so that he may write the very
poem we are reading.

To study Dante is to be an exchange student in his labyrinthine, fully-realized world. I had the advantage of book-
shelves all around me when I was growing up, but many
of you today, accustomed to digital platforms that use language as a throwaway half-thought (tbh), may never have
experienced this phenomenon. Once you do, however, you
never go back. After Dante, the hunger for something real
will never again be satisfied by a mere selfie.

Drawn into Dante's world, readers from all across the
globe, despite social divides, rarely dive into Dante without emerging unaffected. They may be disconcerted by the
grotesque punishments, dazzled by the vibrant images inspired by his *Commedia*, or overwhelmed by the depth of its
characters, places, and core of justice. Online threads pale
in comparison to words like Dante's that are built upon a
bedrock of meaning. When you students read Dante, you
sense something real operating underneath and throughout
the language. You'll thirst for more.

Why Dante?

My interest has always far surpassed my erudition. I'm constantly staggered by the vastness of all I do not know. Yet when I need inspiration or guidance, I always come back to his multi-layered, intoxicating cross-section of stories about power, suffering, love, redemption, and beauty. Read Dante to learn about geometry, geography, poetry, history, and politics. Would that we had a modern-day Dante Alighieri to dive into the cultural abyss and rescue the elixir of meaning! With its emphasis on vision, language, and the perfectly ordered, infinite circles of Creation, the *Commedia* reveals the purpose of his journey, which is not to perceive the plan of the Almighty, but to align our own wills with it and, in turn, reflect this desire in a mimetic, transformative work of poetry.

We who reside in a fractured world find Dante familiar. The broken-hearted poet bestowed upon his world a geometric, joyous thing of beauty to which our own longing and broken souls may return.

Sincerely,

Ms. Gavin

Conclusion: Advice for the Roads

Dear Students,

And that, per Forrest Gump, is all I have to say about that. Thank you for coming along with me this far. Before I go, here is some parting advice; parts of it are likely to rub you the wrong way. Some of it is opinionated, but all of it is sincere.

1. Any time you start a new job, there will be one person who corners you and admonishes mysteriously, "Don't trust *anyone*." Don't trust that person. You want to stay away from people for whom life is an intricate web of plots, alliances, and conspiracies. Leave that to Fortnite.

2. Let people go in traffic. Always assume they are late for a job interview, have to pick up a sick child, or have inside information on a forthcoming typhoon.

3. Cut off toxic people. If you are spending time with someone whose conversation or presence makes you

feel uneasy, uncool, anxious, or doubtful about yourself, it's not you. You're not crazy; don't waste your time. Ask yourself what part of you is getting something out of this relationship, because you can count on it, a part of you is. Let go of that. You want people in your life who inspire you, not deplete you.

4. Stay away from drugs. "Try it, you might like it," they'll insist. Maybe you would. That's exactly the problem. Because now, hello drug habit.

5. Know that the way you are profoundly affects the people around you.

6. Sometimes someone in a store will ask whether you work there. (Isn't that a funny feeling? It's the surprise and amusement. I mean, *Do I actually look like I know what I'm doing?*) They usually want advice of some sort —what time it is, where the bathroom is, which sweater is the best gift for her pre-teen niece. Before shrugging and dodging away, see if you can help them.

7. Perception does not always equal reality. Literature, as we've said, may not mean what you want it to mean. Remember Tennyson's Ulysses, who makes the arrogant claim, "I am a part of all I have known"? How dangerous and egotistical, to look at the world and only see a mirror. Don't force your interpretations on everything around you. Find an inner quiet and just listen.

8. Read books. As many as possible. About anything. Devour them. Don't ever stop practicing your literacy. Read and write. Keep a journal and record your thoughts; don't worry about grammar and making it

"sound good." Write, write, write, and read, read, read. If you don't like to read, you just don't like to read *yet*. You haven't found one that grabs you. *Yet.*

9. Avoid the false high of self-righteousness. Know what your values are, and let your actions every day speak well of them. Understand that people's hearts and minds will never be changed by being coerced to obey a law. Don't try to enforce your personal values strictly, as laws that must be obeyed by everybody around you. It is not your job to punish those who disagree with you, or dismiss them as "closed-minded." Self-congratulatory euphoria with a presumption of being on a higher moral ground than your peers is a dangerous path. It means you've stopped listening and have started policing.

10. Know the difference between wanting to inspire and wanting to be obeyed. One is leadership, and the other is ego.

11. In the professional world, don't wear black leggings as pants, or flip-flops.

12. There will be people who seem perpetually bound to misunderstand you. You might wonder whether it is intentional. Sometimes it will be, but it's no matter. Embrace the linguistic paradigm: we all put things out there. You control your words and actions, so choose them mindfully. You cannot, however, control how they will be received by others. I hope you will someday find this liberating.

13. Acknowledge people who have helped you get where you are. Handwritten cards are best. Write hand-written notes after job interviews, which you should send later the same day.

14. As always, wear your seatbelts and eat your broccoli.

Ahead there, cherubs.

Sincerely,

Ms. Gavin

Appendix

Appendix A
Educational Philosophy

Ms. Gavin

It is important in English class that you take responsibility for your own learning. You are responsible for making your life interesting. Carefully consider the concepts presented. Participate by contributing to class discussions. As with most undertakings in life, your engagement and success in this class will depend on your own level of effort, curiosity, and involvement. Make it interesting for yourself and for the rest of the class—**there is no such thing as a boring idea**. Bored people are simply boring people. They tend to end up old and alone. Hone your curiosity and the ability to engage yourself in the topics we discuss. This skill will come in handy throughout life so you don't wake up one day middle-aged, disillusioned, and headed to a dull job that you loathe in a mind-meltingly wretched manner. Feigning interest often leads to actual enthusiasm, and you will be amazed at what you can learn with a positive attitude.

The thirteenth century Sufi poet Rumi wrote, "Pray for a tough instructor to hear and act and stay within you." Wise man. He also wrote, "Half-heartedness doesn't reach into majesty." For this reason, an apathetic attitude will not help you in this class or in life. Do the reading; don't rely on on-line shortcuts or by asking your friends what happened in last night's chapter. This habit will leave you with stunted literacy; if shortcuts have become your norm, it's no wonder when reading is difficult and unpleasant. Moreover, fake reading will leave you with the deep-down feeling of being a sham. I am not your friend, but I am here to help you think closely about your own learning and help you to become a more literate, well-spoken person.

Too often we fall into the trap of negativity, running down ourselves, our heroes, and the inspiring efforts of those around us. This creates a dangerous and sad type of nihilism that prevents you from discovering the greatness residing within each and every one of you. Your world needs English more than ever. Not only is there an alarming trend of poor public speakers, plunging literacy rates, bad grammar in the media, and lifeless literature, but there is also a widespread lack of belief in the fact that our lives and efforts are meaningful. Because your life **is** meaningful, how you present yourself says a lot about your dignity, integrity, and self-worth.

Sometimes there is more than one right answer; sometimes there are many wrong answers. But being apathetic, half-hearted, or negative is an easy way out. Take the virtuous route and you will reap the personal and educational benefits.

Appendix B
Plagiarism:
ZERO TOLERANCE

Plagiarizing any portion of your work is academic dishonesty. Any assignment you turn in that is not *one-hundred percent your own work* will result in the following consequences:

- Zero on entire assignment.
- Parents contacted.
- Administrative referral.
- Hearing conducted by National Honors Society advisors

THERE ARE NO EXCEPTIONS, AND THIS IS YOUR NOTIFICATION THAT THERE WILL BE NO SECOND CHANCES. THERE IS NO PARTIAL CREDIT. IF YOU GET CAUGHT, THERE WILL BE NO OPPORTUNITY TO RE-DO THE ASSIGNMENT.

No excuse is acceptable, including:

- "I didn't mean to."

- "I was confused/didn't understand."
- "But I changed some of the words around."
- "My parents will e-mail you the reasons I cheated and plead my case."
- "I didn't know it was wrong."
- "I've been really stressed out and didn't have time."
- "My hand accidentally slipped on the right-click button, and then I sneezed and dragged the online passage to my own paper. At that point there was an earthquake, which caused me to right-click again and paste it into my own document. I then changed some of the words around by mistake, but I didn't realize."

Academic dishonesty damages your grade and your reputation.

What about SparkNotes and online summaries?

Online summaries are shortcuts, and poor substitutes for actually reading. They are terribly written and often inaccurate. Online sources will not help you on reading quizzes and tests. If you are confused when you read, it may be because you have been relying for too long on SparkNotes, which are at a fifth-grade reading level. Devote the time and integrity to your assignments, and take pride in your work.

Appendix C
Reading Tips:
Common Problems and Solutions

1. "I can't remember the characters' names or plot details."

Write things down right after you read. Include your personal impressions—force yourself to have opinions on the characters based on what they say, do, wear, eat, and interact with each other. Talk about them with your classmates. Get involved. Start a groupchat. Gossip about the characters relentlessly. Tweet ridiculous memes about them.

When it comes to studying, did you know that the most drastic loss of memory occurs within twenty-four hours of reading something? Review in the morning to refresh your memory. Jot down notes on the insights that arise in class discussions, and you'll see. You'll end up with roadmaps that track a developing idea.

If you come in for extra help, I won't summarize for you. Instead, have your notes in hand so I can help you, see where you may be getting lost, and follow your train of thought.

2. "I can't focus."

Distraction=the millennium. Look, a potato chip!

We all struggle to remain focused. Don't save your reading for right before bed. Block out a chunk of time, not a few minutes here and there. Read in a quiet, comfortable place, free of screens, music, noise, or any other distractions. Don't beat yourself up if you can't focus right away; it takes a while to get into the reading groove. Concentration is a muscle that requires repeated exercise to strengthen. You are not a lost cause.

3. "I read it. My eyes scan. But it doesn't sink in."

We human beings are never too old to be read to. Reading along while you listen to a professional actor performing the lines brings text to life. Sometimes there are musical interludes, or even delightfully cheesy sound effects. However, you must read along. When you read words and hear an actor perform them simultaneously, your eyes won't skim to the bottom of that page; you're kept on pace with the audio. You're activating multiple intelligences and will be more likely to remember what you read long-term.

Appendix D
Essay Comments:
Elizabeth Bishop's "One Art"

Hello, periods four and five. You know our tradition: I read all of your essays, making side notes about strengths, weaknesses, feedback, and samples I'd like to share with you. Below is the list of comments I found myself wanting to write repeatedly. Instead, I have coded them and put those numbers on your paper. A circle is an error. Except for a squiggly underline, whenever something in your paper is checked or underlined, it means your ideas and wording are very effective. Your quiz on these comments will be on Monday.

What a poem! You all kept coming up with incredible insights; how could we possibly limit our ideas to just one day? Time well spent, cherubs.

1. The argument of the paper is what the speaker in the poem feels about loss. What are her tones (attitudes toward the subject)? Have you shown that? "Complex" and "ambivalent" work, but still do not identify the attitudes of the author. In any poem, there are several tones.

Bishop's villanelle structure unravels as her denial becomes harder and harder to sustain. Remember all of the words we had conjured up and discussed. They all work well; use several of them in the introduction and throughout your paper. Using several descriptors of the attitude sets up your essay nicely, especially since the true underlying attitudes are slowly unveiled underneath the initial false ones. There's no hint of remorse or regret here. The poem itself is an attempt to deny the harsh reality of the pain that accompanies life losses. Your introduction should show this in several sentences; it's hard to write an analytical essay that just supports one or two-word arguments.

2. Areas of support. Each body paragraph is an "area of support" because it presents a topic that supports your thesis. Are your areas of support clearly worded? They need to be specifically named, in order, in your thesis statement. Note that the prompt is asking what the tone is, so "tone" on its own doesn't support an argument ("The author uses tone to show tone..."). Each area of support should be more than a word, such as "diction" or "structure." The progression of the objects is a solid area of support, and a lot of people wrote about this exceedingly well! Again, state these areas of support clearly in the thesis statement.

Too broad or vague:
- powerful diction

- unique punctuation
- commentary about art
- repetition
- specific diction
- figurative language
- repeated diction

Successful areas of support for this round of papers included the following noun phrases:

- variations on the polysemous word "love"
- shift in audience from general to specific
- evolution from impersonal to personal language
- revelation about the sublime powers of art
- juxtaposition of tangible and ethereal losses
- diction about location and geography
- concrete and abstract signifiers of time (*wowza!*)
- breakdown of the speaker's poetic composure
- use of the villanelle's structure to detach herself from her emotions
- the motif of movement
- diction about skill to emphasize powerlessness
- progression of items lost—from concrete and impersonal to more significant and personal
- shifting from organized, clearly punctuated statements to disorganized and choppy ideas
- art's power to reveal truth and encourage anagnorisis

Great job on those!

*Be careful; the whole essay should not be a walk-through of what happens in the poem. If you ever find yourself writing, "The poet then goes on to say," then you may be falling into the abyss of Chronological Summary. Few return with little other than a plot.

Se veral of you wrote well about the specific didactic tone of the opening stanzas: "Lose," "accept" and "practice" are all verbs with the understood "you." Syntactically, they are imperatives. They are "how-to" directives, as if the speaker were ordering or instructing someone how to lose because it's not too hard—anyone can do it! (*Insert faux perky smile.*) She slowly moves to the more personal first person. This links to the argument about **tones** quite nicely, and those of you who chose this did marvelously.

Don't forget that each area of support needs to open with a topic sentence that names both the paper's argument and that paragraph's technique.

3. At the end of every body paragraph, make sure you have proven your argument. Remind us (with different phrasing to avoid redundancy) what those attitudes are. Be specific about naming the tones. Use several sentences here, because without this analysis and link to the prompt, the details you have just painstakingly presented turn into summary.

You are probably familiar with my routine of pulling all-nighters to grade essays, and then punctuating my grading with irrelevant procrastinating tasks. I have swept the hallway, flipped through a book about Oscar de la Renta, and smelled various books in the 1920s section of my book shelf. My biggest mistake, however, was deciding to see what all the fuss was about when it comes to who some guy would pick as his wife on "The Bachelor." There was a lot of crying and digital piano music involved. Then I moved on and checked out something called Robot Unicorn Attack. Oh, America, I think I love you!

4. Quote incorporation. Don't use a quotation merely for the purpose of summary; rather, show why that language is important. In an essay this short, it's a disaster to quote more than one line at a time. Trim it and use only what you need.

   For example, if you have quoted "disaster," consider the denotation (dictionary definition) and connotations (the ideas associated in the reader's mind with that word) of the word "disaster." Make sure you break down your cited words closely. A disaster can connote something catastrophic, such as a hurricane or earthquake. Bishop chooses that word for a particular reason, and it connects to the ultimate disaster in the last verse—the one the speaker must acknowledge. What about the word "art"? Art is something that is practiced and requires fine-tuning to reach its full aesthetic potential. Use **double**, not single, quotation marks. Include line numbers.

Only use quotation marks when you are directly citing from the text. If you feel the need to use "air quotes," it probably "means" that you are "aware" that you are using a "cliché" or a "colloquialism" (informal language), so reword the phrase and avoid quotation marks. Using air quotes in writing also sounds condescending for some reason: "Let me put this in language that *you* will understand." The reader feels a patronizing pause when he or she reads air quotes, even though this is far from your intent.

5. Explain this idea further. Before moving on, fully explore your analysis. For example, we mentioned "keys" in class. Keys are small, easily reproducible objects. An hour spent losing them can be annoying, because without them, we cannot enter or secure places closest to our hearts; that could relate to the intense personal connections she opens up to (get it?) later on. Could the whole poem be a key to the truth that the speaker would rather lock away? To get at the underlying meanings that authors place intentionally with their ideas and diction (like Easter eggs), you should analyze each word closely: its denotation, its connotations, and the way it fits in with the writer's purpose.

6. Diction.   Are your words lively and sophisticated? Choose specific words rather than vague phrases. Instead of using "very," pick a better word. For example, instead of writing "very interested," use "fascinated." Instead of "very upset," how about, "devastated"? Words and phrases to avoid: "etc.," "you," "your," "&," "basically," "really," "depressing," "through the use of," and starting sentences with the words "also," "and," and "but." Instead of "due to," opt for "because of." In formal writing, "impact" is not a verb. If you have used "it," what is the "it"? I am getting better and better at Robot Unicorn Attack. They've got dolphins playfully encouraging my unicorn along! I keep thinking this will be the last run, but then I feel so dejected by the cacophonous metallic crash when I fall off a cliff that I yearn to hear Erasure and see the sparkly stars once again.

7. Whenever you are analyzing a poem, you must acknowledge the poetic devices the author has included. You must acknowledge the *poetic devices.* You *must* acknowledge the poetic devices. *You must acknowledge the poetic devices.* Does the poet employ regular rhythm (meter) and rhyme? At the very least, write about whether the poem includes fixed verse or free verse (no regular rhythm or rhyme). Blank verse is unrhymed iambic pentameter—if the poem includes this meter, write about it and connect it to the poem's meaning. If a poem is written in free verse, why might

a poet choose such unrestrained rhythm and meter? While you don't have to make a poetic device an area of support, you should still acknowledge rhythm and rhyme.

From here moving forward, be able to identify the terms from your poetry packet. Review those terms. Sleep with them under your pillow. Laminate them. Serenade them. When you write about the poetry selection on the exam, let the reader know that you are aware that this is a *poem*. Identify the devices throughout your analysis. Now I'm just panicking and making my robot unicorn charge everything. When you make it jump in the air, you hear a narcotic tinkling noise and see pretty colors. It is 2:17 AM.

"One Art" is a villanelle. That structure is **crucial** to the poet's purpose. The structure, along with the speaker's poetic composure, unravels at the very end. Hmmm… could Bishop have chosen one of the most restrictive poetic forms to restrain emotions the speaker would rather bury? The villanelle itself is an attempt to contain the speaker's pain, a truth we feel acutely at the end. "One Art" deliberately fails as a villanelle, but succeeds as a poem. Acknowledge that structure and link it to the poem's message and the speaker's tone.

8. Introduction and conclusion. Both take the lens of the essay and zoom out to show the big picture and uni-

versal human lessons. Get philosophical! In a few sentences, explain how reading the passage this way illuminates or enhances the writer's themes. In the conclusion, think about what universals the reader can understand or appreciate further (about human nature, catharsis, grief, writing, etc.) from analyzing the passage in this way. Not all literature is a call to action, so don't boil the work down to a treacly moral ("She is saying we need to live life to the fullest."). What profound statement is Bishop making about the art of denial, and the art of poetry? What is art's purpose, and is it served here? How does art take on a power and life of its own?

9. Snappy titles! Incorporate the author's name. You guys outdid yourselves with creative titles, even if they were wacky. I appreciate that you went there. Not that you'd submit these titles in formal essays, but here are some period four and five titles of distinction: The Art of Writing a Well-Developed Essay in Forty Minutes Isn't Too Hard to Master, Though It May Look Like (Say it!) a Sham, Bishop's Bummer [oy vey!], Lost but Never Found, Nobody Is the Boss of Loss, Bishop's Death-match with Denial, Mosaic of Memories, Bishop's Art in Check, and A Successful Failure of Poetry.

Appendix E
Dante and the Price
of Beguiling Rhetoric

Dear Students,

I'm including an essay for you here so you can see a sample of academic writing. I was inspired to write it for the St. John's College graduate program. It's flawed, but know that I'm putting it out there not expecting it to be perfect. Life lesson! Moreover, I wanted to show you a paper that relies mostly on original sources, or "core texts," as we Johnnies call them. I don't cite modern articles, but I have used Robert Durling, Allen Mandelbaum, and Mark Musa's translations and notes. Mark Musa is where I first encountered the Book of James allusions, and many other scholars have also made the James connection. You'll know what I mean if you read it.

So there you have it. And now you will find an essay on what Dante has to say about charming wordsmiths and the lies they tell themselves.

Fondly,

Ms. Gavin

* * *

Smooth talkers. They get away with everything.

In Dante's *Inferno*, the evil counselors are obscured in flames in the eighth circle, a fitting contrapasso for the scathing obfuscations of truth the sinners have committed in their mortal lives. Fire is polysemous here; in the Book of James, chapter 3, the writer compares the tongue to both a fire and to a ship, as one has the potential for quick and widespread destruction, while the other can be steered by a small rudder of "great pretensions." Canto 26 relates the episode of the travelers' encounter with Guido da Montefeltro, who recounts the tale of his condemnation and steadily proclaims his innocence.

We might wonder why these sinners are placed in a circle lower than that of adultery, suicide, and even murder, yet closer scrutiny reveals a schism within the souls of those who have distributed fraudulent advice. Most of the shades in Hell have failed to view their place in the cosmos in the correct proportions, but as James 3 tells us, teachers are judged more harshly because of the precious nature of their obligations. Reflecting on Guido da Montefeltro's episode teaches us about the rightful conduct of advisors, who must give just counsel while tempering their humility; Dante's depiction of Guido will also enlighten readers about the good and just view of language, a sacred gift not to be abused.

Initially, Guido da Montefeltro's voracious hunger to hear about the world of men is palpable. From the writhing flame in which he is now enclosed, Guido begs for information about his home country, "burning" for news about who is in power (line 24). His request to speak with Dante about politics is, like his punishment itself, a form of thinking that devours him, yet being in Hell would seem to render this information irrelevant. Preoccupation with power and fame is part of what has condemned Guido, whose concern for mortal recognition knows no restraint.

In lines 37 through 54, Dante answers Guido's question about Romagna and relays a multitude of information about contemporary Italian politics. His six tercets depict a country that is not at war with another nation, but with itself, divided into turfs patrolled by usurpers. Dante's diction ("war," "tyrants," "broods," "pinions," "trial," "bloody heap," "claws," "mastiffs," "drills teeth," "changes alliance," and "lion") accurately describes the brutal behavior of power-hungry men. Dante's tropes of animalistic violence depict the manner in which these men have disregarded reason, unleashing their appetites for supremacy and, ultimately, rendering them slaves to their ruthless desires.

We would think that such behavior would obviate life on earth as unpalatable, yet Guido is not willing to detach himself from it; he still prizes its sanction. Recounting the mortal events that led up to his condemnation, Guido boasts

> The tricks and the hidden ways, I knew them all,
> and I so plied their art that the fame of it went out
> to the ends of the earth. (76-8)

Instead of probing the cause of his self-inflicted fall, Guido is almost bragging about his former vices, even ones he claims to have relinquished at his end-of-life "conversion." Guido's statement about his fame reveals a secular assessment of human value that he has not quite renounced. His currency quantifies accomplishments by the frequency with which one's name is spoken by others. Not only is Guido hungry for current information about Italian politics in the world above, but he is also measuring success by worldly benchmarks—the opinions of the living—instead of his standing with God.

For all of his self-absorption, Guido da Montefeltro lacks true self-reflection and cannot acknowledge his error. He is certain that he would have been saved because of his repentance,

> had it not been for the high priest, may evil take
> him! who put me back into my first sins;
> and how and qua re,
> I wish you to hear from me. (70-72)

The four tercets (lines 85-96) in which Guido emphasizes the Pope's villainy, calling him "[t]he prince of the new Pharisees," comprise a significant amount of speech devoted to blaming somebody else, particularly when articulation from within the flame requires so much pain and labor. Guido's castigation of Boniface even exceeds blaming, for his interjectory curse ("may evil take him!") belies his previous self-characterization as a victim, instead revealing his own fatal misunderstanding about his place in the world. The power of judging and damning souls is not for Guido to wield, nor is he a sieve of experience by which all actions are judged.

After censuring the Pope, he tells Dante that the details of his story are something "I wish you to hear from me," so eager to prove his blamelessness that he commandeers his legend, anxious to counter any false stories about him that may be roaming the earth. Ironically, Guido is never named here, nor is Ulysses. Names, like fame and reputation, are earthly phenomena. The only naming that is of worth to God is the naming He does himself, beginning with Creation in the Old Testament.

When Dante presses Guido about his identity, wanting to hear his story of ignominy, Guido replies,

> If I believed that my reply was to a person who
> would ever return to the world, this flame would
> remain without further shaking;
> but since never from this depth has any one
> returned alive, if I hear the truth, without fear of
> infamy I answer you. (61-66)

Guido makes abysmal judgments based on what he hears, both here and with Pope Boniface VIII later on. He is engrossed by identity, but only his own: it does not occur to him to ask about Dante's physicality or occupation. Relying on his own wits, Guido assumes his superior reason is a self-contained unit that is independently capable of discovering truth. Little does Guido know that he is speaking to a great living poet: one who is learning about the right way to God, who will return to the corporeal world, and whose poetic endeavors will surely proliferate Guido's name.

In assuming that those whom he encounters in Hell are all permanent residents, Guido underestimates God. His concerns are social, not spiritual; so captivated by his own "fear of infamy" and caring more for his own prideful *kleos* than for true salvation, Guido misses the palpable truth that is standing before him.

Heightened self-absorption and an inflated sense of human importance obscure the divine, leaving Guido susceptible to fallacies that take him further away from God. Throughout the *Commedia* we are reminded to keep our perceptions—of ourselves, of our place in the world, and of God—in the proper proportions. When we confer so much weight to earthly glory, our sight becomes riveted to earthly bodies, limiting our understanding to material substances.

Guido's language about geography expresses his fixation on the physical world. He speaks of the "sweet Italian earth from whence I bring all my guilt" (26), as if the soil itself, not his own soul, were the source of the guilt which accompanies him externally on his descent. In describing the countryside of his birth, he says he was "from the mountains there between / Urbino and the ridge whence Tiber is unleashed" (29-30). Guido's pride may be boundless, but his geographical schema admits of borders presented by the landscape. Were Guido to see properly, however, he would realize that his topography omits God. In fact, his characterization of the Tiber as a cord unleashed is stated in the passive voice, attributing no agency to a prime mover.

Psalm 129 properly venerates nature's vastness: "How precious to me are your designs, O God; how vast the sum of them!" (Ps 139, 17)[1] Dante's *Inferno* is full of shades who attempt to justify their sin, but to "justify" also means here to assign boundaries, and to determine an ethical code of right and wrong. Nature is mighty and immense, as are human desires, but it is up to God to demarcate the limits of human behavior. Guido's name, he boasts, went "to the ends of the earth," but this is beyond where men's names should journey.[2]

Like Manichean blasphemy, Guido's concentration on the earthly realm takes root in his fixation on the universe's physicality. Hell is infused with cacophonous stimuli that punish the senses in a constant barrage of synesthesia, replicating the corporeal concerns of the shades' former lives. Each level of Hell is undeviating in its fixed system of impervious circles, motes, and pockets.

Purgatorio, however, suggests a diaphanous permeability of the terraces leading to Heaven, as the souls do penance for their sins and become lighter, drifting through ethereal peripheries to the next level. Their wills ultimately surprise them as they purify themselves and refine their vision to a sublime moment of self-selecting ascension. Guido would have seen the tangible gates of Hell on his way to the eighth circle, but has clearly missed the meaning of the words inscribed therein.

Guido's alignment with corporeal bodies leaves him more vulnerable to the Pope's claim of possessing the ability to lock and unlock the gates of Heaven at will. The Pope's allusion to the keys of Heaven are compelling to Guido, who has prioritized the world of men over the realm of God to such an extreme that he spends his afterlife in a world circumscribed by opaque perimeters and corporeal punishments. Dante emphasizes Hell's rigidity in the last lines of Canto 27, when Dante and Virgil reach the "next arch, which covers the / ditch where the toll is collected" (134-5) by the next level of shades. God has placed these boundaries throughout His designs so that humans may know their place and view their lives in correct proportion.

Our living clay is overseen by the hand of Providence, since, as Psalm 139 declares, "You formed my inmost being; you knit me in my mother's womb" (Ps 139, 13). Yet Guido misspeaks when, referring in passing to his origin, he speaks of a time when he "was the form of bone and flesh that my / mother gave me" (73-4). Still confined to the world of carnality, Guido ascribes his existence to his mother, not to God. A more traditional translation of the Psalm reads

> For thou hast possessed my reins: thou hast protected me from my mother's womb. I will praise thee, for thou art fearfully magnified: wonderful are thy works, and my soul knoweth right well. My bone is not hidden from thee, which thou hast made in secret: and my substance in the lower parts of the earth. (Douay-Rheims, Ps 138, 13-15)

In this reading, God's work on a new life is one of restraint, as He curbs the flesh from its very inception, thereby protecting it in this hidden process. The gospel of John says of true believers that they "were born not by natural generation nor by human choice nor by a man's decision but of God" (John 1, 13). Guido's portrayal of his in utero life offers no tribute to God, nor does it differentiate a human being from any other creature in the animal kingdom.

Rousseau's "natural man" answers to no one, enjoying his freedom in the abundant natural environment, but in Dante's world, men without restraint are dangerous and wild creatures, as evidenced by both Dante's tropes of wild animals battling on Romagna's political stage and in Guido's description of his former cunning ways as the works "of a fox" (75). People who do not restrain their passions or acknowledge God are brutish, fighting among themselves and pacing the earth restlessly, animated by their own physical desires. [3]

Grounded in (and by) his vocabulary of the physical world, Guido uses tropes of disease to describe his encounter with Boniface. After characterizing the Pope's words as "drunken" (99), Guido claims that the Pope requested Guido to "teach him / to recover from his proud fever" (96-7). This random piece of fiction evidences Guido's eagerness to portray himself as a spiritual doctor ministering to the people rather than a conniving consigliere. Such claims are counterproductive to Guido's attempts to authenticate his innocence. In fact, they only call attention to the sin in Guido's lapse of judgment, for he later swears by the compelling reason of Boniface's argument.

If we are to believe him here, then Guido has sinned because he has heeded the feverish words of a plainly drunk and delusional man. His eloquence would seem to make such foolishness unlikely, yet if we are to discredit what he says here about the Pope's condition, then we are ascribing to him the fraud that he attempts to displace on others. Both options validate Guido's rightful place in the circle of fraud.

Guido misallocates the author of life and therefore does not acknowledge the perimeters within which his actions should have abided. He thinks he is telling Dante a story of transformation, and in a sense this is true: he mentions five different types of array that have clothed him. First he is enfolded in his mother's womb, then in the arms of a military career, and then, the last of his mortal life, in the cord and robes of a Franciscan friar. Upon his death, he is encoiled within the wrathful tail of Minos, and finally, is hidden within a burning flame. Guido says that, upon his death, the black cherubim "seized" him and carried him down to Minos (121), but Guido does not depict being carried here as being swaddled in clothing. Being carried by the demon may be a dark parody of Guido's earlier image (being carried by his mother), or it may emphasize Guido's efforts to characterize himself as a passive victim.[4] If Guido viewed his life's garments correctly, as sacred vestments circumscribed by God,[5] then he would have several opportunities for true transformation, resulting in an appropriate perception of God as the Prime Mover.

Proper recognition of God's strictures positions the world's concrete objects in their due perspectives, as they are symbolic representations of divine creation. True words are expressions of our intentions, but the words of the fraudulent are disposable castoffs that do not match their insidious purposes, thus their counterfeit. Guido's account of his "repentance" is that he became a Franciscan, "believing, so girt, to make amends" (68). This belief is his downfall, for he speaks more of the outward signs of atonement than of true remorse for his actions.

Because Guido is limited to the world of physicality, his cords do not signify authentic penitence and are thus reduced to theatrical props. A Franciscan cord curbs his waist, but not his natural desires. Guido's synecdoche, wherein he invokes a concrete part of his orders as opposed to the sublime whole, belies his meaningless oath when he says that, in making him sin, the Pope did not "[regard] in me the rope that used to make its / wearers thinner" (91-3). Guido's figurative language exposes his failed attempt to align his internal and external vestments. His sincerity becomes even more suspicious when he says of his conversion, "and it would have worked" (Mandelbaum translation, line 84) had the Pope not intervened. Describing the success or failure of an action to bring about a desired outcome in terms of "working" highlights the superficiality of the undertaking. Guido speaks of his plan in the hyperbolic language of a caricatured evildoer, as if he were an impetuous mustache-twirling villain: Rats—foiled again!

Words in the possession of the disingenuous are, like empty gestures, showy but blank hoaxes. Such a language arsenal renders Dante's opening analogy in lines 7-15 of canto 26 quite appropriate:

> As the Sicilian bull, which first bellowed with the
> cries of him—and that was right—who had
> tempered it with his file,
> used to bellow with the voice of the afflicted one,
> so that, though made of brass, still it seemed

transfixed with pain:
so, not having any path or outlet from its origin
within the fire, the anguished words
were converted into its language.

The bronze bull is designed to distort and amplify the sounds of the roasting human hidden within, just as the flames of the fraudulent counselors mangle the language of the shades into grotesque utterances. The instrument of torture is created to make a masterpiece out of human suffering, and the first victim it consumes is its creator, who has manipulated his sculpting genius to create a tool of destruction. To similarly devastating ends, Guido has "so plied" the "art" of cunning (77). Both masterminds are punished, consumed by the talent they have abused in their lifetimes.

Canto 26 emphasizes the de-civilizing force that language, improperly exercised, forces on its users; far from expressing the pious desires of a prayerful community, the bull emits inarticulate sounds of agony. The metonymy of the Sicilian bull is a monstrous inversion of the womb, an image Guido evokes incidentally sixty-one lines later. Hidden in the dark recesses of the bull is not the mystery of a budding soul, but a human perishing in misery. Its creator is a false god who has "tempered" his creation, not so that it will be curbed or restrained properly, but so that the instrument can amplify the sounds of anguish within. The bronze instrument is not the seat of creation's miracle, but a dastardly enclosure that destroys human life and makes a spectacle of the suffering it inflicts.

The sculptor gifts his invention to a man he knows to be a cruel leader, just as Guido places his knowledge in the possession of a corrupt usurper with sinister designs. In the possession of the unjust leader, the bull becomes a showpiece of cruelty for public entertainment. Guido has also crafted a polished exterior and, with his Franciscan garb, makes a show of conversion, substituting the external symbols of artificial conversion for true repentance and leaving his soul vulnerable to exploitation by tyrants.

The bull's beastly utterances are garbled transmissions removed from the source of its hideous cries, fitting since Guido has demonstrated the price of separating words from their meaning. Dante replicates this phenomenon in the scene of Guido's fall from grace, when Pope Boniface VIII uses devious language to pry military advice from Guido. Attempting to assuage Guido's fear of Hell, Boniface purrs, "Let not your heart fear: / henceforth I absolve you, if you teach me how to / raze Palestrina to the ground" (100-2), but such a promise calls attention to itself, like the braying bull, for its hollow falsity.

A master manipulator, the Pope has appealed to Guido's fear, an emotion he can deduce from Guido's late repentance. Guido has unwittingly revealed the same to us earlier, in telling Dante he may speak without "fear of infamy." Guido's fright returns at his death, when the black cherub claims him, snatching his body possessively: "O wretched me! how I trembled when he seized me" (121-2). A lifetime of uneasiness suppressed by word tricks resurfaces in this terrifying moment. Guido's apprehension is well-placed, for he has accepted an illogical bargain, willingly suspending his reason to give the Pope the advice he seeks. Even were he not a Franciscan friar, Guido, having already boasted about knowing the crafty ways of men, should know better than to accept this absurd promise.

In this moment of decision, Guido ignores several obvious premises. The very nature of the request, to raze an entire city to the ground, should cast suspicions on the Pope and his bombastic promises of salvation. One of Guido's charges in his opening invective against Boniface is that he fights unjust wars against fellow Christians, yet the Pope is seeking advice for how to demolish Palestrina, a city that poses no threat to Christendom.[6]

By boasting that his recommendation will help the Pope "triumph / on your high throne" (110-1), Guido is acknowledging the Pope's motivation for worldly power, once again enticed by the world of human authority and using phrasing more appropriately reserved for the adoration of God. Guido knows where repentance lies, for when he retires from a violent military career, he does not seek out the warring Pope to make amends, rather he takes holy orders. Furthermore, by accepting Guido's advice (to offer Palestrina's citizens false amnesty), the Pope is exposing a duplicity that Guido freely overlooks. In offering a recommendation that, when heeded, renders the recipient a liar, Guido ignores common sense and embraces the impossible a priori absolution offered by a treacherous fiend.

Initially, the eighth circle may seem to be the incorrect circle for Guido da Montefeltro, for in this canto we are likely to consider Pope Boniface, like Ulysses, to be the more fraudulent counselor who prioritizes his own power over the soul of his subjects. After all, the advice Guido gives is, unfortunately for Palestrina, accurate: by breaking promises to the city, the Pope is able to annihilate it. Guido is telling the Pope to lie, but is not giving the Pope false counsel; rather, the fraud in this canto is the one Guido tells himself in rationalizing the breaching of his holy orders. The betrayal of his holy vows is made more abhorrent because his counsel advances deceit, but this abdication of virtue is another iteration of Guido's attempts to justify a moral code outside of God's will. In doing so, he becomes, like the victim of the Sicilian bull, a creator meeting his downfall because of his own (ad)vice.

Guido's inhumane counsel perpetuates a chain of broken trust. Not only does he brag about having knowledge of the ways of men, but Guido also transmits that information to a tyrant. He perceives Palestrina's good faith as a vulnerability, exploiting a social and spiritual attribute that is crucial to forming bonds with fellow men and with God. The third chapter of the book of James teaches that

> the tongue is a small member and yet has great pretensions. Consider how small a fire can set a huge forest ablaze. The tongue is also a fire. It exists among our members as a world of malice, defiling the whole body and setting the entire course of our lives on fire, itself set on fire. (5-6)

James' words elucidate the nature of this circle's punishment, and also speak to the cosmic sweep of language's power. Guido never mentions remorse for the sadistic violence wrought upon the innocent civilians of Palestrina, nor for the fact that, because of his five words ("lunga promessa con l'attender corto"), an entire city is brutally destroyed, punished because of its virtue.[7]

Even the lowest beasts of Hell recognize the logic that Guido denies, for at the moment of his death, a black cherub arrives to claim his soul (surprise!), shooing away St. Francis and exclaiming,

> Do not take him,
> do not wrong me.
> He must come down among my slaves, because
> he gave the fraudulent counsel, since when, until
> now, I have been at his locks;
> for he cannot be absolved who does not repent,
> nor can one repent and will together, because of
> the contradiction, which does not permit it. (112-118)

As he carries Guido to Hell, the demon sneers, "Perhaps you did not think I was a / logician!" (122-3). Guido has suspended Aristotle's principle of non-contradiction, a concept residing at the basement of all knowledge and comprehended by even the most despicable of fiends. When Guido reaches Minos, who assigns him his proper place in the circle of fraudulent counselors, Minos' body becomes a grotesque and fearsome declaration, yet it expresses the justice that God has created.

We may feel sympathy for Guido in his pitiable state, but must remember that High Justice is the artificer of Hell, and, as the inscriptions on the gates of Hell attest, Guido's punishment is righteous. Guido's misstep is a refusal of basic logic, but is also sinful because it contradicts Christian theology.

Pope Boniface's claim to be able to absolve someone of a sin before it is committed is a leap in the sequence of time, and only God resides outside of time.

In the first part of his *Summa Theologicae*, St. Thomas of Aquinas distinguishes God's eternity from man's sense of a temporal reality, clarifying that "[e]ternity is altogether at once. But in time there is before and after" (Question 10 Article 4). Thomistic theology holds that revelations about the essence of God only come when we are released from the physical world, and that revelation, being a whole, happens "at once" (Question 12, Article 10). With his spurious and prideful claims, Boniface has disregarded not only the ropes of the Franciscan order, but also the metaphysical restraints of time and space. As a mortal and a Catholic, the Pope disobeys the sequence of events to which his corporeality limits him.

Guido blasphemes in calling Pope "Father," for he is acknowledging the feigned vestiture of God's power that the Pope has donned. In addressing him thus and agreeing to the impossible fallacy, Guido is legitimizing the Pope's behavior, not surprising considering his fixation on the sanction of men.

Through language, we can attempt to close the divide that exists between each other and between God and ourselves. We cannot, however, say something is so and thereby make it so. Only God can do that, which relegates Dante's fraudulent counselors to cheap imitators. God's word, not limited to a mere sign for a corresponding reality, is what it claims to be, and is. Mentors who abuse language visit damage to the social fabric by punishing the faith that is necessary for salvation, thus are punished themselves for their mistaken view of the universe and their place in it.

The fraudulent counselors not only punish their subjects, but also offend God with sinful tokens of feeble mimicry. Guido da Montefeltro's erroneous, heightened sense of his own importance in the cosmos is a cause of his condemnation. When he tells Dante of becoming a friar in an attempt to atone for his past, he claims that, were it not for the Pope's meddling, "surely [his] / belief would have been fulfilled" (68-9). Guido's certainty is misplaced, as the power of fulfilling beliefs and turning a thought into a truth is restricted to God.[8] Pope Boniface VIII's blasphemous promise and posturing as God, along with Guido's complicity in flouting human limitations, indicts them both.

In *Confessions*, Augustine recollects the youthful indiscretion of stealing from a pear tree, elaborating on why such a seemingly minor incident is actually a disastrous calamity. He tells God

> All men mount a grotesque imitation of you when they set you at a distance in order to exalt themselves above you. Yet even in this mimicry of you they indicate that it is you, the creator of all nature, they would be, and they cannot extract themselves from that nature. [Was pear theft a sin because I was] enacting a prisoner's maimed freedom, breaking rules where punishment did not reach, in a shadowy pretense at being able to do anything I want? (Book 2, chapter 2, section 14)

In *Inferno's* Canto 27, both Pope Boniface VIII and Guido da Montefeltro abuse their gifts by usurping the vastness of creation and answering to nothing but their own self-congratulation.

Guido turns the eye of blame on another, too prideful to resist sharing his privileged knowledge. Because his external gestures are not aligned with internal intentions of piety, he is assaulted by ironies that he desperately tries to ignore. God's words are not meant to evade meaning, or, like the Pope's promise of salvation that actually condemns, denote the exact opposite of what they say. God is conscious of truth that is consistent throughout all levels of being and understanding, whereas Guido is not. Guido's opening words upon approaching Dante, for example, after he has seen Ulysses depart, indicate a fervent desire to speak with the travelers, "though I have arrived perhaps somewhat late" (22). Readers are aware of Guido's late-life conversion and may be struck by his last-minute, after-death abduction by the dark angel. In apologizing for his lateness, however, Guido does not know how accurate he is, and misses the significance of his own words.

Saint Augustine tells God in Book 11, after emphasizing that God does not reside in time as we know it,

> your Word does not fade our or follow in sequence, it is immortal and eternal. Therefore it is with a Word that is eternal that you utter, all at once and for all time, all things you utter, and whatever you utter comes to be. And it comes to be by nothing but your utterance. (Chapter 2, section 9)

Only God would be able to forgive a sin before it is committed (were He to wish it), and only He can create something by declaring it. In Genesis, God says so, thereby making it so.

In the first verse in the gospel of John it is written, "In the beginning was the Word, and the Word was with God, and the Word was God." In the world of men, words are causes of emotion, thought and action. In God's Word, however, the cause equals the effect, a luminous miracle of semantic apotheosis. Here there is no verbal irony, but Guido's actions and speech are full of contradictions, rendering Guido divided, like feuding Romagna and Christendom under Pope Boniface's tyranny, against himself. For Guido's penitence to be complete, his transformation would have to be thorough, from the inside out, yet he only brandishes the external signs of salvation, doing damage to the trusting and creating a semiotic disconnect. This polysemous fracture exhibits symptoms on several levels: the fissure of symbols and referents, the hypocrisy of his faux conversion, the victims of his fraud being punished for their virtue, and, finally, the permanent rift between God and himself.

For such a complex sin, Dante devises a fitting contrapasso for the fraudulent counselors, who now must struggle to do what they once did glibly. Being ensconced in a flame is the flawlessly balanced punishment, for, as Virgil explains to Dante, "Within the fires are the spirits; each is swathed in / that which burns him inwardly" (26. 47-8). God's perfection is such that, in *Inferno*, where the souls' sins are literalized, His creations exhibit external appearances that perfectly match the condition of the interior.

For all of the difficulty and "anguish" that speaking from the flame presents, the souls are still plagued by the urge to speak. The counselors who took advantage of their superior knowledge and used it as an excuse to disregard God's boundaries are now confined. Instead of living out the magnitude for which they hungered in life, they are now limited, disembodied voices dissociated from their names and likenesses. In the first lines of Canto 27, Virgil dismisses the once mighty Ulysses' flame like a teacher dismissing a naughty schoolchild, and it trundles off, wandering away because its story has ended.

Guido's flame is more restless in its writhing and flickering, first attracting the travelers' notice because of the "confused sound" (5) emanating from its peak. For all of Guido's pride, which has unmoored his words from their anchor of their significance, he has now been reduced to a wisp of fire, and one can only identify him by close scrutiny of his labored, subversive language. He will find no peace in the flame that will burn until the end of time, and he departs, not quieted as is the flame of Ulysses, but with more tempestuous thrashing, exclaiming that he torments himself. Throughout the canto, Dante describes the Guido da Montefeltro's contorted motions eight times, and as Guido is still not acknowledging God or giving credit to God's justice, his flame will continue to whip about fiercely in perpetuity.

What, then, is the proper use of speech? James' assessment of the tongue as a dangerous weapon that can misguide a life's entire course provides a grave warning, and Dante's twenty-seventh canto actually provides several examples of language that is administered appropriately. The brief utterances of Virgil's discharge of Ulysses and Minos' judgment are in keeping with God's will; they each speak to the higher order of the world, thus are good and true. Dante the Poet's simile of the deadly Sicilian bull, while dangerously poetic, is edifying, for it guides its reader to a better mental image of the contrapasso and culminates in an act that Dante classifies as "just."

Because we do not have God's extemporal capacity for literalizing our words, we must use figurative language, metaphors wherein one item stands for another. Guido's metonymy of his Franciscan rope fails because it is reductive, minimizing an entire system of holy beliefs to a single object significant to Guido only because of its concrete existence. Dante's analogy of the bronze bull, however, is expansive, serving as hypertext that adds to our understanding of God's cosmos. As Robert Durling reminds, the third chapter of James indicates that

> [i]f anyone does not fall short in speech, he is a perfect man, able to bridle his whole body also. If we put bits into the mouths of horses to make them obey us, we also guide their whole bodies. (2-3)

The verbal restraint Dante attempts when he first enters the eighth circle ("I rein in my wit more than / is my custom, / that it may not run without virtue guiding it," lines 20-2) is the fitting bridle that virtuous men ought to apply to their speech. At the moment of Guido's death, in the startling standoff between St. Francis and the fallen angel, Francis remains tacit. He departs when he hears the demon's argument, for while the declaration may be shocking and distasteful to readers, Francis recognizes that it is true. Guido's initial silence when the Pope approaches him is just and good, but his discipline is defeated by the paradoxical allure of simultaneous superiority and salvation.

Here Dante presents a variation on his behavior in earlier episodes of *Inferno*. After previous encounters with shades, Dante (both Poet and Pilgrim) deliberated with Virgil or expounded on the significance of the scene and its emotional impact on him. This time, when Guido concludes his story and departs, the Pilgrim is notably silent. Rather than debriefing and conferring with Virgil about what he has just heard, Dante says nothing and proceeds to the next level. Dante's silence here proves to be a newly-emerging form of healthy discipline. His reticence marks a wise and refreshing deviation from the beginning of the same canto, where he is so eager to tell Guido what he knows about the politics of Romagna that he delivers a speech of his own, "already prepared" (34).

In an address lasting more than twenty lines, Dante's parade of gossip is a sign that he has fallen prey to the same paradigm that has doomed Guido: he is proud of the exclusive knowledge that only he possesses, and is eager to be the superior individual who relays information to a recipient who so fervently desires it. Dante's silence when Guido has finished speaking is juxtaposed with the commotion of Guido's flame, but it also indicates that, because he quietly absorbs the lesson in what he has just heard, Dante has just practiced the virtue of curbing his language.

As the first words of James 3 admonish,

> Not many of you should become teachers, my brothers, for you realize that we will be judged more strictly, for we all fall short in many respects. (1-2)

It is sinful to use one's talent to gain advantage in the worldly system of social hierarchy; therefore, the fraudulent counselors have fallen because they have made false gods out of their own skills. They entice men to follow them in the name of knowledge, but only for the purpose of reveling in their exalted status as mortals. These leaders are judged so harshly because, instead of serving man and God, shepherding their followers to virtue, they engage in false puppetry.

In this episode of *Inferno*, Dante makes us all too aware of our vulnerability to charismatic but insincere word-crafters, whose vacant priorities and deceptive words shred the tapestry of human kinship. Their advice is divisive to the social fabric because they are themselves somehow divided. Such treachery corrupts the state, but, in contrast, James 3 asserts

> the wisdom from above is first of all pure, then peaceable, gentle, compliant, full of mercy and good fruits, without inconstancy or insincerity. And the fruit of righteousness is sown in peace for those who cultivate peace. (17-8)

The same chapter also reminds us that a spring cannot "gush forth from the same opening both pure and brackish water" (11), which explains why words from murky souls such as Guido's and Boniface's would be non-potable.

Guido da Montefeltro's fate demonstrates the perils of words divorced from the truth. Such a separation of signifiers and the signified is acrimonious indeed, for words stripped of meaning can become throwaway half thoughts (omg! lol!) or weapons in the hands of master marketers who re-draw the boundary lines of ethics, telling fallible mortals what we want to hear, not what we need to hear, about our proper place in Creation.

Who among us is unmoved by charismatic and well-timed words for which we pine, particularly if they promise to rescue us from the worst fears and suspicions we have about the condition of our own souls? Guido's destiny teaches us, and Dante, about aligning our talents with God's will and resisting the dangerous allure of pretty lies that from the mouths of authoritative sources. Heeding the advice of deceitful counselors estranges us from God, while true and good mentorship is an instrument of the divine that can teach us about humility, peace and piety in a cosmos ordained by a loving God.

* * *

[1] All Biblical citations, unless otherwise noted, are from the New American Bible. Mark Musa points out the passage from James in his translation of *Inferno*.

[2] Ulysses, another sinner in the circle of fraudulent counselors, also does not respond virtuously to nature's enormous scale, instead seeing it as a challenge, the terrain as something to be conquered. He too presses natural limits, even changing his boat into an aircraft with oars for wings.

[3] In the previous canto, Ulysses appeals to his men by saying, "[Y]ou were not made to live / like brutes, but to follow virtue and knowledge" (26. 118-9), yet his rhetoric so inflames his men that they lose their reason. He cannot hold them back, and they embark on a "mad flight" (125).

[4] This ironic gesture of carrying also shadows another that has occurred in Canto 23. After being tricking by the Malebranche, Virgil flees the bolgia grasping Dante "instinctively…like a mother waking to some warning sound, [who] grabs her son and runs…she cares not for herself, only for him" (Musa translation, 37-40). This image is not merely a gripping depiction of a narrow escape; it is an icon of selfless familial care—something about which the black cherubim knows nothing. He too snatches his charge, but only because he is eager to deliver him into the arms of torment.

[5] Psalm 139 reads, "Behind and before you encircle me and rest your hand upon me" (5).

[6] The sin of creating divisiveness among Christians is punished later in *Inferno*, and in the last line of this canto, Dante and Virgil move to their next destination, where are punished "those who gain cargo by putting apart" (27, 136).

[7] After the words "high throne," Guido skips the rest of his life's story to the moment of his death, an abrupt leap in time. In the previous canto, Ulysses' story ends with his death, and we do not hear about his afterlife. Perhaps this speaks to Ulysses' concerns as a pagan epic hero of the classical world. We learn that, since the moment of Guido's fall, a black angel has been eagerly waiting to take him to Hell; presumably any subsequent life works are irrelevant and garner him no salvation. It is still odd that Guido does not relay any information about the rest of his life; one wonders if he could have truly repented in his lifetime. Guido's account to Dante, however, indicates that he has not allowed himself to acknowledge his suspension of judgment. Such an admission would require self-reflection, and none of the shades in *Inferno* exercise that faculty.

[8] Guido repeats the words of others three times in the canto: Virgil's dismissal of the Ulysses/Diomedes flame, Pope Boniface VIII's argument and the fallen angel's claim on his soul. In Hell, he can only repeat the words of authority figures who are all limited themselves, while not actually having any power himself. Unlike Guido's previous influence, he is now incarcerated in a flame and stuck with duplicate language.

Works Cited

Aquinas, Thomas. *The Treatise on the Divine Nature: Summa Theologica I* 1—13.Trans. Brian J. Shanley, O.P. Indianapolis: Hackett Publishing Company, Inc., 2006. Print.

Augustine, St., Bishop of Hippo. *Confessions*. Trans. Garry Wills. New York: Penguin Group, 2006. Print.

Durling, Robert, Translator. *Inferno*[1]. By Dante Alighieri, Oxford University Press, 1997. Print.

Mandelbaum, Allen, Translator. *The Divine Comedy: Inferno, Purgatorio, Paradiso.* By Dante Alighieri, A.A. Knopf, 1995. Print

Musa, Mark, Translator and Editor. *Indiana Masterpiece Editions: Dante's Inferno, The Indiana Critical Edition.* By Dante Alighieri, Indiana UP, 1995. Print.

---

[1] n.b. I've selected specific translations of Dante's *Inferno* to best suit various segments of the paper. To avoid confusion, the three version of Dante's *Inferno* I've cited are listed alphabetically by their translators. Augustine's *Confessions*, however, is listed by the author.

Acknowledgements

In a book about teaching, not thanking the teachers who inspired me would be an unthinkable omission. Thank you to Mrs. Paull, Ms. Capone, Mr. Mac (Don't throw the helmets), Mme. Beaton (Bonjour, flaunt it), Ms. McCabe (Sippin' cider through a straw), Mr. Schauble (People who can find inspiration in hard times—that's noble), Mr. MacDonald (SABKACKMP), Ms. Giudici (Come on, guys), Mrs. Baxter, Ms. Kyles (Good morning to you), Ms. Volat (Hail to the Redskins), Mr. Waxman, Ms. Vallee, Ms. Steckler (Let the music inspire your writing), Mr. Rousseau (Take it from the top), Mr. and Mrs. Lindia, Terry and Linda Shanley, Ms. Dallek, Ms. Yahia, and Mme. McLeod.

Thank you to institutions that inspired me and created my most formative moments: the University of Mary Washington, St. John's College in Annapolis, and the National Endowment for the Humanities. Thank you Bill Stephany, Ronald "Big Ron" Herzman, Wes Kennison, and Lynn Melizzi Kennison. Thank you to the Dallas Institute of Humanities and Culture, especially Glenn Arbery, Claudia Allums, and Larry Allums. Most likely you don't remember me, but I often remember you with fondness and gratitude.

Thank you to students who bring themselves fully to class every day with character and grace, without pretensions, and who try, try, try. Thank you to Eastchester's school administrators and colleagues for your support, and to the Eastchester community for your warmth.

Hey Lolly, you crazy-ass abando-dog.

Thank you to my heroic Dad whose love and strength surpass words. Thank you to dear sweet Dolores who shoved ice cream under the bed in elementary school before confessing to Dad, and who will never fathom just how much I look up to her. And to Bruce, who is my Atticus Finch, Joe Hackett, and Gary Cooper all rolled up into one. I am one lucky gal.